3rd May 1989

FAITH

Compiled by ICOREC
Edited by Martin Palmer, Anne Nash and Ivan Hattingh

Original illustrations by
Miles Aldridge, Mike Nicholson, Rachel Ross and Chris White

AND NATURE

Century
London   Melbourne   Auckland   Johannesburg

Co-published with the WWF UK

A Rider Book published in the Century
Paperback series by Century Hutchinson Ltd,
Brookmount House, 62–65 Chandos Place,
Covent Garden, London WC2N 4NW

Century Hutchinson Australia (Pty) Ltd
PO Box 496, 16–22 Church Street,
Hawthorn, Melbourne, Victoria 3122

Century Hutchinson New Zealand Ltd
32–34 View Road, PO Box 40–086,
Glenfield, Auckland 10

Century Hutchinson South Africa (Pty) Ltd
PO Box 337, Bergvlei 2012, South Africa

Designed by Andrew Gossett/Omnific Studios

Set in Monophoto Poliphilus and Blado by
Balding + Mansell International Limited

Printed and bound in Great Britain by
Kogan Page Ltd

British Library Cataloguing in Publication Data

Palmer, Martin
  Faith and nature: our relationship with the
natural world explained through sacred literature
  1. Human ecology—Religious aspects
  I. Title   II. Nash, Anne   III. Hattingh,
Ivan
  291.1'78362   GF80

ISBN 0 7126 1921 6

CONTENTS

6   INTRODUCTION

10   SELECTIONS FROM THE SCRIPTURES

40   PRAYER AND PROSE

52   PILGRIMAGE FOR LIFE

60   SELECTIONS FROM THE DECLARATIONS

70   THE ASSISI CEREMONY

78   STORIES, MYTHS AND LEGENDS

92   REFERENCES TO THE TEXT

95   ACKNOWLEDGEMENTS

96   ABOUT THE WORLD WILDLIFE FUND

       CONTACT ADDRESSES

INTRODUCTION

We, members of major world religions and traditions, and men and women of good will, are gathered here, in this marvellous Church of St Francis, to awaken all people to their historical responsibility for the welfare of Planet Earth, our Sister and Mother, who in her generous sovereignty feeds us and all her creatures.

With these words Father Lanfranco Serrini, Minister General of the Franciscans (OFMConv) opened the historic gathering of members of different faiths and members of many conservation organisations on the 29th September 1986. The occasion was the 25th Anniversary of the World Wide Fund for Nature International (WWF). The venue was the Basilica of St Francis in Assisi, Italy – birthplace and burial place of the Roman Catholic patron saint of ecology. The reason was simple, yet staggeringly vast in its consequences: namely, to bring the worlds of faith, with their powerful traditions about how we should relate to nature, into active contact with the worlds of secular and scientific conservation, with their urgent message about how close to the edge we are currently living.

At Assisi, on that windy yet warm day in late September 1986, each of the major faiths proclaimed through liturgy, scripture, symbol and final Declarations, where they stood on the issue of conservation. Likewise, the secular forces of conservation looked into their own values and beliefs and began to realise that there was more to this world than they had ever dreamt possible. From this came the new Network on Conservation and Religion – an international programme of action, reflection and education in which, for the first time ever, each of the major faiths dedicated itself to developing, within the integrity of their own beliefs, action on the environment. This network is now active in many parts of the world, and you can join it by writing to the address given at the end of the book.

This book has grown out of the work done leading up to Assisi, as well as drawing upon material and insights which have surfaced through the network. It is a celebration of the deep and moving truths which lie within all the major faiths of our world. Yet we do not offer this as some simplistic syncretism: for just as in the biological world, so also in the world of beliefs and values, diversity is vital. As Father Serrini said in his introduction at Assisi:

We are convinced of the inestimable value of our respective traditions and of what they can offer to re-establish ecological harmony; but, at the same time, we are humble enough to desire to learn from each other. The very richness of our diversity lends strength to our shared concern and responsibility for our Planet Earth.

There can be no question but that ecology needs the spiritual dimension to bring it to a fullness and a depth which can make the salvation of the physical world a reality. Yet it is also true that, should these fine words of the faiths remain just that, religion will have failed in its divinely given responsibility to awaken all people to their responsibility for and with nature. It is in this spirit that we offer the insights, visions, hopes and beliefs which this volume contains.

There are four sections with too few pages and there is much which we have had to leave in the hope of further volumes. We have concentrated on the five faiths – Buddhism, Christianity, Hinduism, Islam and Judaism – which were represented at Assisi. Three other faiths made considerable contributions to the events at Assisi and we have therefore included some material from these faiths. The Baha'is joined in fully and have since Assisi begun work on their own Declaration, to be issued late in 1987; the Sikhs were instrumental in helping to run the event and particularly the Retreat; traditional Chinese belief has proved one of the most important sources, especially with regard to children's work arising from 'Worlds of Difference', the WWF UK book on religion and conservation which launched this whole new network.

There are other faiths, such as the Jains and the Zoroastrians, which have much to offer in this area. Likewise aboriginal and indigenous cultures such as the Maoris and native North Americans have profound insights to share. Our space however is limited, and to include material from all of these faiths and traditions would not have allowed us to do justice to any of them. We hope to be able to cover these other traditions in a further volume. We ask your forgiveness for that which is not here and your enjoyment of that which is.

The first section covers scriptural sources. In the cases of Judaism, Christianity and Islam, the Hebrew Bible, the New Testament and the Qur'an are the sources we have turned to. Christians will find that material taken from what they know as the Old Testament is contained in the Jewish section. For the scriptures of Hinduism and Buddhism, the Sikhs and the Baha'is, we have drawn upon the vast corpus of materials available, and have been guided in our selection by scholars and activists from each faith. In all cases this is but a taste of what the scriptures have to offer on the theme of faith and nature. We offer them as signs, hints of the greater depths which are there for all to explore if they so wish.

For the second section we have drawn upon classical prose and poetry. Much of this comes from the commentaries, reflections and meditations of great 'saints' within each faith. The directness and clarity with which this interprets the broader scriptural or traditional teachings can often speak with tremendous power to us as we look at how we, in this age, should respond to these teachings.

The third section presents material from the WWF International Event at Assisi. Here, for the first time in history, five of the world's main faiths (Buddhism, Christianity, Hinduism, Islam and Judaism) stated categorically how each faith stood on the question of ecology. From this arose the Five Declarations, one from each faith, spelling out what it meant to follow that particular faith and how this should shape the believer's relationship with nature. Through meditation, liturgy, teaching and Declaration the five faiths explored, side by side but within their own traditions, what they could say to a world bent on ecological suicide. From this we have drawn that which we feel provides much ground for reflection, prayer and action.

Finally we have included an all too brief selection of some stories, myths and legends from the faiths. In these stories we can encounter a deeper reality if we allow ourselves to be spoken to by the pictures which these stories can paint for us. They can impart very simply a message which we often fail to encounter in reality or fact.

The texts given fall into two main types. There are texts which speak directly about how we should treat the world around us because of what we hold to be true. There are also texts which, by reflection upon the true nature of both the divine and the natural, show how all of life is caught up in the Ultimate, and that no part of it is without value and meaning. We have tried as far as possible to avoid the use of the natural world as metaphor or simile. While such usage can be interesting in its own right, it has little to offer to our understanding of our relationship with the natural world, having more to do with our understanding of the religious teachings.

Whilst species and ecosystems are our main concern, it is worth remembering that we lose daily, through development, 'westernisation' or genocide, ancient patterns of life, with deep spiritual roots. The urgent need to see beliefs and values as part of threatened ecosystems is beautifully if tragically captured in the words of a Yanomamo leader. The Yanomamo have lived in balanced relationship with the Amazonian forests for millennia. In the last ten to fifteen years however, virtually all of this has been destroyed by the exploitation of the forest and the destruction – often deliberate – of the Yanomamo people:

Everyone likes to give as well as to receive. No-one wishes only to receive all the time. We have taken much from your culture . . . I wish you had taken something from our culture . . . for there were some good and beautiful things in it.

Whether you will use this book for personal devotion; reflection or meditation; for preparing worship or assemblies; for teaching or preaching; for action and commitment; we ask you to come prepared to give and to receive. In the words of Father Serrini at Assisi:

Let us now, each according to the wealth of our own religious tradition, celebrate our common concern for the future of the world.

SELECTIONS FROM THE SCRIPTURES

BUDDHISM

Surely if living creatures saw the results of all their evil deeds, they would turn away from them in disgust. But selfhood blinds them, and they cling to their obnoxious desires. They crave pleasure for themselves and they cause pain to others; when death destroys their individuality, they find no peace; their thirst for existence abides and their selfhood reappears in new births. Thus they continue to move in the coil and can find no escape from the hell of their own making. And how empty are their pleasures, how vain are their endeavours! Hollow like the plantain-tree and without contents like the bubble. The world is full of evil and sorrow, because it is full of lust. Men go astray because they think that delusion is better than truth. Rather than truth they follow error, which is pleasant to look at in the beginning but in the end causes anxiety, tribulation, and misery. [1]

*

Speak the truth, do not yield to anger; give if you are asked; by these three steps you will become divine. Let a wise man blow off the impurities of his self, as a smith blows off the impurities of silver, one by one, little by little, and from time to time.

    Lead others, not by violence, but by righteousness and equity. He who possesses virtue and intelligence, who is just, speaks the truth, and does what is his own business, him the world will hold dear. As the bee collects nectar and departs without injuring the flower, or its colour or scent, so let a sage dwell in the community. [2]

*

"I preach the Dharma to beings whether their intellect
Be inferior or superior, and their faculties weak or strong.
Setting aside all tiredness,
I rain down the rain of the Dharma.

When I rain down the rain of the Dharma,
Then all this world is well refreshed.
Each one according to their power take to heart
This well-preached Dharma, one in taste.

As when it rains the shrubs and grasses,
The bushes and the smaller plants,
The trees and also the great woods
Are all made splendid in the ten regions;

So the nature of Dharma always exists for the weal of the world,
And it refreshes by this Dharma the entire world.
And then, refreshed, just like the plants,
The world will burst forth into blossoms. [3]

Now at that time the Exalted One dwelt near Rajagaha, in the Bamboo Grove, at the Squirrels' Feeding-Ground. And at that time the Retreat during the rainy season was not yet appointed for the brethren by the Exalted One. So the brethren went a-roaming in the cold, and hot, and the rainy seasons alike.

Thus folk were vexed and murmured angrily, saying: What! Are the recluses who are the sons of the Sakyan to roam about in the grass, they crush the living thing that has one sense, they trample to death many a tiny life.

Are the recluses of the heretical sects, who follow a Norm illpreached – are they to settle down and live retired during the rains? Are birds to build their nests on the tree-tops and take shelter in the rains and live retired, and yet are the recluses who are the sons of the Sakyan to go a-roaming in the cold, the hot, and the rainy season alike, treading down the green grass, crushing the living things that one sense, trampling to death many a tiny life?

Now some brethren heard those folk who were vexed and murmured angrily thus, and they told the thing to the Exalted One.

Therefore in this connection and on this occasion, the Exalted One, after a pious talk, thus spake unto the brethren:

I enjoin on you, brethren, that ye observe the retreat during the rains. [4]

A Bodhisattva resolves: I take upon myself the burden of all sufferings, I am resolved to do so, I will endure it. I do not turn or run away, do not tremble, am not terrified, nor afraid, do not turn back or despond.

And why? At all costs I must bear the burdens of all beings, in that I do not follow my own inclinations. I have made the vow to save all beings. All beings I must set free. The whole world of living beings I must rescue, from the terrors of birth, of old age, of sickness, of death and rebirth, of all kinds of moral offence, of all states of woe, of the whole cycle of birth-and-death, of the jungle of false views, of the loss of wholesome dharmas, of the concomitants of ignorance – from all these terrors I must rescue all beings . . . . I walk so that the kingdom of unsurpassed cognition is built up for all beings. My endeavours do not merely aim at my own deliverance. For with the help of the boat of the thought of all-knowledge, I must rescue all these beings from the stream of Samsara, which is so difficult to cross, I must pull them back from the great precipice, I must free them from all calamities, I must ferry them across the stream of Samsara. I myself must grapple with the whole mass of suffering of all beings. To the limit of endurance I will experience in all the states of woe, found in any world system, all the abodes of suffering. And I must not cheat all beings out of my store of merit. I am resolved to abide in each single state of woe for numberless aeons; and so I will help all beings to freedom, in all the states of woe that may be found in any world system whatsoever.[5]

Creatures without feet have my love,
And likewise those that have two feet,
And those that have four feet I love,
And those, too, that have many feet.

May those without feet harm me not,
And those with two feet cause no hurt;
May those with four feet harm me not,
Nor those who many feet possess.

Let creatures all, all things that live,
All beings of whatever kind,
See nothing that will bode them ill!
May naught of evil come to them![6]

*

Spread with garlands af kareri, the regions of the earth are delightful.
    Resounding with elephants those lovely rocks delight me.
Those rocks delight me, the colour of blue clouds, beautiful, cool with water,
    having pure streams, covered with Indagopaka insects.
Like the ridge of a blue cloud, like an excellent gabled house, resounding with
    elephants those lovely rocks delight me.
The lovely surfaces are rained upon; the mountains are resorted to by seers.
    Made to resound by peacocks, those rocks delight me.
It is enough for me, desiring to meditate, resolute, mindful. It is enough for me,
    a resolute bhikku desirous of the goal.
It is enough for me, a resolute bhikku desirous of comfort. It is enough for me,
    a resolute venerable one, desirous of application of mind.
Being covered with flax flowers as the sky is covered with clouds, full of flocks of
    various birds, those rocks delight me.
Not filled with householders, but resorted to by herds of deer, full of flocks of various
    birds, those rocks delight me.
With clear water and wide crags, haunted by monkeys and deer, covered with
    ooozing moss, those rocks delight me.[7]

Long ago, brahman Dhamika, rajah Koranya had a king-banyan tree called steadfast, and the shade of its widespread branches was cool and lovely. Its shelter broadened to twelve leagues – none guarded its fruit and none hurt another for its fruit.

Now then came a man who ate his fill of fruit, broke a branch and went away. Thought the god dwelling in that tree: "How astonishing it is, that a man should be so evil as to break a branch off the tree, after eating his fill. Suppose the tree were to bear no more fruit."

And the tree bore no more fruit.[8]

*

There comes a time when, sooner or later, after the lapse of a long, long period, this world passes away. And when this happens, beings have mostly been reborn in the World of Radiance; and there they dwell, made of mind, feeding on rapture, self-luminous, traversing the air, continuing in glory; and thus they remain for a long, long period of time. There comes also a time when, sooner or later, this world begins to re-evolve. When this happens, beings who had deceased from the World of Radiance usually come to life as humans. And they become made of mind, feeding on rapture . . . and remain thus for a long, long period of time . . .[9]

*

CHRISTIANITY

Note: For Old Testament quotes turn to Judaism sections

That is why I am telling you not to worry about your life and what you are to eat, nor about your body and how you are to clothe it. Surely life means more than food, and the body more than clothing! Look at the birds in the sky. They do not sow or reap or gather into barns; yet your heavenly Father feeds them. Are you not worth much more than they are? Can any of you, for all his worrying, add one single cubit to his span of life? And why worry about clothing? Think of the flowers growing in the fields; they never have to work or spin; yet I assure you that not even Solomon in all his regalia was robed like one of these. Now if that is how God clothes the grass in the field which is there today and thrown into the furnace tomorrow, will he not much more look after you, you men of little faith? So do not worry; do not say, "What are we to eat? What are we to drink? How are we to be clothed?" It is the pagans who set their hearts on all these things. Your heavenly Father knows you need them all. Set your hearts on his kingdom first, and on his righteousness, and all these other things will be given you as well. [10]

*

In the beginning was the Word, and the Word was with God, and the Word was God. He was in the beginning with God; all things were made through him, and without him was not anything made that was made. In him was life, and the life was the light of men. The light shines in the darkness, and the darkness has not overcome it. [11]

*

I think that what we suffer in this life can never be compared to the glory, as yet unrevealed, which is waiting for us. The whole creation is eagerly waiting for God to reveal his sons. It was not for any fault on the part of creation that it was made unable to attain its purpose, it was made so by God; but creation still retains the hope of being freed, like us, from its slavery to decadence, to enjoy the same freedom and glory as the children of God. From the beginning till now the entire creation, as we know, has been groaning in one great act of giving birth; and not only creation, but all of us who possess the first-fruits of the Spirit, we too groan inwardly as we wait for our bodies to be set free. For we must be content to hope that we shall be saved – our salvation is not in sight, we should not have to be hoping for it if it were – but, as I say, we must hope to be saved since we are not saved yet – it is something we must wait for with patience. [12]

*

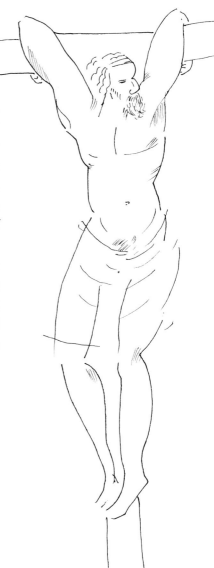

Then I saw a new heaven and a new earth; the first heaven and the first earth had disappeared now, and there was no longer any sea. I saw the holy city, and the new Jerusalem, coming down from God out of heaven, as beautiful as a bride all dressed for her husband. Then I heard a loud voice call from the throne, 'You see this city? Here God lives among men. He will make his home among them; they shall be his people, and he will be their God; his name is God-with-them. He will wipe away all tears from their eyes; there will be no more death, and no more mourning or sadness. The world of the past has gone.'

Then the One sitting on the throne spoke: 'Now I am making the whole of creation new' he said. 'Write this: that what I am saying is sure and will come true.' And then he said, 'It is already done. I am the Alpha and the Omega, the Beginning and the End. I will give water from the well of life free to anybody who is thirsty; it is the rightful inheritance of the one who proves victorious; and I will be his God and he a son to me.' [13]

*

. . . . . The time has come to destroy those who are destroying the earth. [14]

*

HINDUISM

There was at first no Being – nor blank.
There was no air, nor sky beyond.
What was in it? Where?
In whose protection?
Was water there, deep beyond measure?
There was no death, nor deathless state,
No night, no day.
The One breathed, without breath by its own power.
There was nothing else; no, nothing else.
Darkness lay wrapped in darkness.
All was water, all, all over.
Love began, at first; desire was the seed of mind.
Sages and poets, searching within,
saw the link of Being in non-Being.
But who really knows? Who can tell –
How it was born, where creation began?
The gods came later: Who then knows.
That from which creation came.
Whether founded well or not.
He who sees from heaven above.
He only knows. Or, He too knows it not![15]

*

The god of creation, who in the beginning was born from the fire of thought before the waters were; who appeared in the elements and rests, having entered the heart:
This in truth is That.

The goddess of Infinity who comes as Life-power and Nature; who was born from the elements and rests, having entered the heart:
This in truth is That.

Agni, the all-knowing god of fire, hidden in the two friction fire-sticks of the holy sacrifice, as a seed of life in the womb of a mother, who receives the morning adoration of those who follow the path of light or the path of work:
This in truth is That.

Whence the rising sun does come, and into which it sets again; wherein all the gods have their birth, and beyond which no man can go:
This in truth is That.

What is here is also there, and what is there is also here. Who sees the many and not the ONE, wanders on from death to death.

Even by the mind this truth is to be learned: there are not many but only ONE. Who sees variety and not the unity wanders on from death to death. [16]

*

As fire, though one, takes new forms in all things that burn, the Spirit, though one, takes new forms in all things that live. He is within all, and is also outside.

As the wind, though one, takes new forms in whatever it enters, the Spirit, though one, takes new forms in all things that live. He is within all, and is also outside.

As the sun that beholds the world is untouched by earthly impurities, so the Spirit that is in all things is untouched by external sufferings.

There is one Ruler, the Spirit that is in all things, who transforms his own form into many. Only the wise who see him in their souls attain the joy eternal. [17]

*

His Being is the source of all being, the seed of all things that in this life have their life. He is beyond time and space, and yet he is the God of forms infinite who dwells in our inmost thoughts, and who is seen by those who love him.

He is beyond the tree of life and time, and things seen by mortal eyes; but the whole universe comes from him. He gives us truth and takes away evil, for he is the Lord of all good. Know that he is in the inmost of thy soul and that he is the home of thy immortality.

May we know the Lord of lords, the King of kings, the God of gods: God, the God of love, the Lord of all.

We cannot see how he works, or what are the tools of his work. Nothing can be compared with him, and how can anything be greater than he is? His power is shown in infinite ways, and how great is his work and wisdom!

No one was before he was, and no one has rule over him; because he is the source of all, and he is also the ruler of all.

May God who is hidden in nature, even as the silkworm is hidden in the web of silk he made, lead us to union with his own Spirit, with Brahman.

He is God, hidden in all beings, their inmost soul who is in all. He watches the works of creation, lives in all things, watches all things. He is pure consciousness, beyond the three conditions of nature, the ONE who rules the work of silence of many, the ONE who transforms one seed into many. Only those who see God in their soul attain the joy eternal.[18]

*

OM. In the centre of the castle of Brahman, our own body, there is a small shrine in the form of a lotus-flower, and within can be found a small space. We should find who dwells there, and we should want to know him.

And if anyone asks, 'Who is he who dwells in a small shrine in the form of a lotus-flower in the centre of the castle of Brahman? Whom shall we want to find and to know?' we can answer:

'The little space within the heart is as great as this vast universe. The heavens and the earth are there, and the sun, and the moon, and the stars; fire and lightning and winds are there; and all that now is and all that is not: for the whole universe is in Him and He dwells within our heart.'[19]

*

I am the sweet fragrance in earth and the brilliance in fire, the life in all beings, and I am austerity in the austere.

Know Me, O Partha, as the eternal seed of all beings; I am the intelligence of the intelligent. The splendour of the splendid (things and beings), am I.

He who hates no creature, who is friendly and compassionate to all, who is free from attachment and egoism, balanced in pleasure and pain, and forgiving,

Ever content, steady in meditation, self-controlled, possessed of firm conviction, with mind and intellect dedicated to Me, he My devotee is dear to me. [20]

*

Untrammeled in the midst of men, the Earth, adorned with heights and gentle slopes and plains, bears plants and herbs of various healing powers. May she spread wide for us, afford us joy!

On whom are ocean, river, and all waters, on whom have sprung up food and ploughman's crops, on whom moves all that breathes and stirs abroad – Earth, may she grant to us the long first draught!

To Earth belong the four directions of space. On her grows food; on her the ploughman toils. She carries likewise all that breathes and stirs. Earth, may she grant us cattle and food in plenty!

On whom the men of olden days roamed far, on whom the conquering Gods smote the demons, the home of cattle, horses, and of birds, may Earth vouchsafe to us good fortune and glory! . . . . .

All creatures, born from you, move round upon you. You carry all that has two legs, three, or four. To you, O Earth, belong the five human races, those mortals upon whom the rising sun sheds the immortal splendor of his rays.

May the creatures of earth, united together, let flow for me the honey of speech! Grant to me this boon, O Earth.

Mother of plants and begetter of all things, firm far-flung Earth, sustained by Heavenly Law, kindly and pleasant is she. May we ever dwell on her bosom, passing to and fro! . . . . .

Whatever I dig of you, O Earth, may you of that have quick replenishment! O purifying One, may my thrust never reach right into your vital points, your heart!

Your circling seasons, nights succeeding days, your summer, O Earth, your splashing rains, your autumn, your winter and frosty season yielding to spring – may each and all produce for us their milk! . . . . .

When at the Gods' command, O Goddess, you unfurled yourself, revealing your grandeur, then you were imbued with beauty and charm. You shaped and fashioned the world's four regions.

In village or forest, in all the places where man meets man, in market or forum, may we always say that which is pleasing to you! . . . . .

May your dwellings, O Earth, free from sickness and wasting, flourish for us! Through a long life, watchful, may we always offer to you our tribute!

O Earth, O Mother, dispose my lot in gracious fashion that I be at ease. In harmony with all the powers of Heaven set me, O Poet, in grace and good fortune![21]

*

ISLAM

Behold, thy Lord said to the angels: "I will create a vicegerent on earth." They said, "Wilt Thou place therein one who will make Mischief therein and shed blood? – whilst we do celebrate Thy praises and glorify Thy holy (name)?" He said: "I know what ye know not."

And He taught Adam the nature of all things; then He placed them before the angels, and said: "Tell Me the nature of these if ye are right."

They said: "Glory to Thee: of knowledge we have none, save what thou hast taught us: in truth it is Thou who art perfect in knowledge and wisdom."

He said: "O Adam! tell them their natures." When he had told them, Allah said: "Did I not tell you that I know the secrets of heavens and earth, and I know what ye reveal and what ye conceal?"[22]

*

Behold! In the creation of the heavens and the earth, and the alternation of Night and Day, – there are indeed Signs for men of understanding, –
Men who celebrate the praise of Allah, standing, sitting, and lying down on their sides, and contemplate the (wonders of) creation in the heavens and the earth, (with the thought): "Our Lord! not for naught hast Thou created (all) this! Glory to Thee! Give us salvation from the Penalty of the Fire.[23]

There is not an animal (that lives) on the earth, nor a being that flies on its wings, but (forms part of) communities like you. Nothing have we omitted from the book, and they (all) shall be gathered to their Lord in the end.[24]

*

He has created the heavens and the earth for just ends: far is He above having the partners they ascribe to Him.

He has created man from a sperm-drop; and behold this same (man) becomes an open disputer!

And cattle He has created for you (men): from them ye derive warmth, and numerous benefits, and of their (meat) ye eat.

And ye have a sense of pride and beauty in them as ye drive them home in the evening, and as ye lead them forth to pasture in the morning.

And they carry your heavy loads to lands that ye could not (otherwise) reach except with souls distressed: for your Lord is indeed Most Kind, Most Merciful:

And (He has created) horses, mules, and donkeys, for you to ride and use for show: and He has created (other) things of which ye have no knowledge.

And unto Allah leads straight the Way, but there are ways that turn aside: if Allah had willed, He could have guided all of you.

It is He who sends down rain from the sky: from it ye drink, and out of it (grows) the vegetation on which ye feed your cattle.
With it He produces for you corn, olives, date-palms, grapes and every kind of fruit: verily in this is a Sign for those who give thought.

He has made subject to you the Night and the Day; the Sun and the Moon; and the Stars are in subjection by His Command: verily in this are Signs for men who are wise;

And the things on this earth which He has multiplied in varying colours (and qualities); verily in this is a Sign for men who celebrate the praises of Allah (in gratitude).

It is He who has made the sea subject, that ye may eat thereof flesh that is fresh and tender, and that ye may extract therefrom ornaments to wear; and thou seest the ships therein that plough the waves, that ye may seek (thus) of the bounty of Allah and that ye may be grateful.

And He has set up on the earth mountains standing firm, lest it should shake with you; and rivers and roads; that ye may guide yourselves;
And marks and sign-posts; and by the stars (Men) guide themselves.

Is then He who creates like one that creates not? will ye not receive admonition?[25]

*

(Allah) Most Gracious is firmly established on the throne (of authority).
To Him belongs what is in the heavens and on the earth, and all between them, and all beneath the soil.
If thou pronounce the word aloud, (it is no matter): for verily He knoweth what is secret and what is yet more hidden.
Allah! there is no god but He! To Him belong the Most Beautiful Names.[26]

*

And He it is Who makes the Night as a Robe for you, and Sleep as Repose, and makes the Day (as it were) a Resurrection.

And He it is Who sends the Winds as heralds of glad tidings, going before His Mercy, and We send down purifying water from the sky –

That with it We may give life to a dead land, and slake the thirst of things We have created – cattle and men in great numbers.

And We have distributed the (water) amongst them, in order that they may celebrate (our) praises, but most men are averse (to aught) but (rank) ingratitude.[27]

Not without purpose did We create heaven and earth and all between! That were the thought of Unbelievers! but woe to the Unbelievers because of the Fire (of Hell)!

Shall We treat those who believe and work deeds of righteousness, the same as those who do mischief on earth? Shall we treat those who guard against evil, the same as those who turn aside from the right? [28]

*

See ye not how Allah has created the seven heavens one above another,
And made the moon a light in their midst, and made the sun as a (Glorious) Lamp?
And Allah has produced you from the earth, growing (gradually),
And in the End he will return you into the (earth), and raise you forth (again at the Resurrection)?
And Allah has made the earth for you as a carpet (spread out),
That ye may go about Therein, in spacious roads. [29]

*

Then let man look at his Food (and how We provide it):
For that We pour forth Water in abundance,
And we split the earth in fragments,
And produce therein Corn,
And Grapes and nutritious Plants,
And Olives and Dates,
And enclosed Gardens, dense with lofty trees,
And Fruits and Fodder, –
For use and convenience to you and your cattle. [30]

JUDAISM

Note: this also covers Christian Old Testament material

And the Lord took man and put him in the Garden of Eden, to tend it and guard it. [31]

*

And the name that Adam gave to each living being has remained its name forever. [32]

*

God blessed Noah and his sons, saying to them, 'Be fruitful, multiply and fill the earth. Be the terror and the dread of all the wild beasts and all the birds of heaven, of everything that crawls on the ground and all the fish of the sea; they are handed over to you. Every living and crawling thing shall provide food for you, no less than the foliage of plants. I give you everything, with this exception: you must not eat flesh with life, that is to say blood, in it. I will demand an account of your life-blood. I will demand an account from every beast and from man. I will demand an account of every man's life from his fellow men.
"He who sheds man's blood, shall have his blood shed by man, for in the image of God man was made."
As for you, be fruitful, multiply, teem over the earth and be lord of it.'
    God spoke to Noah and his sons, 'See, I establish my Covenant with you, and with your descendants after you; also with every living creature to be found with you, birds, cattle and every wild beast with you: everything that came out of the ark, everything that lives on the earth. I establish my Covenant with you: no thing of flesh shall be swept

away again by the waters of the flood. There shall be no flood to destroy the earth again.'

God said, 'Here is the sign of the Covenant I make between myself and you and every living creature with you for all generations: I set my bow in the clouds and it shall be a sign of the Covenant between me and the earth. When I gather the clouds over the earth and the bow appears in the clouds, I will recall the Covenant between myself and you and every living creature of every kind. And so the waters shall never again become a flood to destroy all things of flesh. When the bow is in the clouds I shall see it and call to mind the lasting Covenant between God and every living creature of every kind that is found on the earth.'

God said to Noah, 'This is the sign of the Covenant I have established between myself and every living thing that is found on the earth.'[33]

*

If, when attacking a town, you have to besiege it for a long time before you capture it, you must not destroy its trees by taking an axe to them: eat their fruit but do not cut them down. Is the tree in the fields human that you should besiege it too?[34]

*

Where were you when I laid the earth's foundations?
Tell me, since you are so well-informed!
Who decided the dimensions of it, do you know?
Or who stretched the measuring line across it?
What supports its pillars at their bases?
Who laid its cornerstone
When all the stars of the morning were singing with joy,
and the Sons of God in chorus were chanting praise?
Who pent up the sea behind closed doors
when it leapt tumultuous out of the womb,
when I wrapped it in a robe of mist
and made black clouds its swaddling bands;
when I marked the bounds it was not to cross
and made it fast with a bolted gate?
Come thus far, I said, and no farther:
here your proud waves shall break.

Have you ever in your life given orders to the morning
or sent the dawn to its post,
telling it to grasp the earth by its edges
and shake the wicked out of it,
when it changes the earth to sealing clay
and dyes it as a man dyes clothes;
stealing the light from wicked men
and breaking the arm raised to strike?
Have you journeyed all the way to the sources of the sea,
or walked where the Abyss is deepest?
Have you been shown the gates of Death
or met the janitors of Shadowland?
Have you an inkling of the extent of the earth?
Tell me all about it if you have!
Which is the way to the home of the light,
and where does darkness live?
You could then show them the way to their proper places,
or put them on the path to where they live!
If you know all this, you must have been born with them,
You must be very old by now!

Have you ever visited the place where the snow is kept,
or seen where the hail is stored up,
which I keep for times of stress,
for days of battle or war?
From which direction does the lightning fork
when it scatters sparks over the earth?
Who carves a channel for the downpour,
and hacks a way for the rolling thunder,
so that rain may fall on lands where no one lives,
and the deserts void of human dwelling,
giving drink to the lonely wastes
and making grass spring where everything was dry?
Has the rain a father?
Who begets the dewdrops?
What womb brings forth the ice,
and gives birth to the frost of heaven,

when the waters grow hard as stone
and the surface of the deep congeals?

Can you fasten the harness of the Pleiades,
or untie Orion's bands?
Can you guide the morning star season by season
and show the Bear and its cubs which way to go?
Have you grasped the celestial laws?
Could you make their writ run on the earth?
Can your voice carry as far as the clouds
and make the pent-up waters do your bidding?
Will lightning flashes come at your command
and answer, 'Here we are'?
Who gave the ibis wisdom
and endowed the cock with foreknowledge?
Whose skill details every cloud
and tilts the flasks of heaven
until the soil cakes into a solid mass
and clods of earth cohere together?
Do you find a prey for the lioness
and satisfy the hunger of her whelps
when they crouch in their dens
and lurk in their lairs?
Who makes provision for the raven
when his squabs cry out to God
and crane their necks in hunger?[35]

I look up at your heavens, made by your fingers,
at the moon and stars you set in place –
ah, what is man that you should spare a thought for him,
the son of man that you should care for him?

Yet you have made him little less than a god,
you have crowned him with glory and splendour,
made him lord over the work of your hands,
set all things under his feet.

sheep and oxen, all these,
yes, wild animals too,
birds in the air, fish in the sea
travelling the paths of the ocean.

Our Lord, how great your name throughout the earth![36]

*

Bless the Lord, my soul.
O Lord my God, how great you are!
Clothed in majesty and glory,
wrapped in a robe of light!

You stretch the heavens out like a tent,
you build your palace on the waters above;
using the clouds as your chariot,
you advance on the wings of the wind;
you use the winds as messengers
and fiery flames as servants.

You fixed the earth on its foundations,
unshakeable for ever and ever;
you wrapped it with the deep as with a robe,
the waters overtopping the mountains.

At your reproof the waters took to flight,
they fled at the sound of your thunder,
cascading over the mountains, into the valleys,
down to the reservoir you made for them;
you imposed the limits they must never cross again,
or they would once more flood the land.

You set springs gushing in ravines,
running down between the mountains,
supplying water for wild animals,
attracting the thirsty wild donkeys;
near there the birds of the air make their nests
and sing among the branches.

From your palace you water the uplands
until the ground has had all that your heavens have to offer;
you make fresh grass grow for cattle
and those plants made use of by man,
for them to get food from the soil:
wine to make them cheerful,
oil to make them happy
and bread to make them strong.

The trees of the Lord get rain enough,
those cedars of Lebanon he planted;
here the little birds build their nest
and, on the highest branches, the stork has its home.
For the wild goats there are the mountains,
in the crags rock-badgers hide.

You made the moon to tell the seasons,
the sun knows when to set:
you bring darkness on, night falls,
all the forest animals come out:
savage lions roaring for their prey,
claiming their food from God.

The sun rises, they retire,
going back to lie down in their lairs,
and man goes out to work,
and to labour until dusk.
O Lord, what variety you have created,
arranging everything so wisely!
Earth is completely full of things you have made:

among them vast expanse of ocean,
teeming with countless creatures,
creatures large and small,
with the ships going to and fro
and Leviathan whom you made to amuse you.

All creatures depend on you
to feed them throughout the year;
you provide the food they eat,
with generous hand you satisfy their hunger.

You turn your face away, they suffer,
you stop their breath, they die
and revert to dust.
You give breath, fresh life begins,
you keep renewing the world.

Glory for ever to the Lord!
May the Lord find joy in what he creates,
at whose glance the earth trembles,
at whose touch the mountains smoke![37]

*

Let heaven praise the Lord: praise him, heavenly heights,
praise him, all his angels, praise him, all his armies!

Praise him, sun and moon, praise him, shining stars,
praise him, highest heavens, and waters above the heavens!

Let them all praise the name of the Lord, at whose command they were created;
he has fixed them in their place for ever, by an unalterable statute.

Let earth praise the Lord: sea-monsters and all the deeps,
fire and hail, snow and mist, gales they obey his decree,

mountains and hills, orchards and forests,
wild animals and farm animals, snakes and birds,

all kings on earth and nations, princes, all rulers in the world,
young men and girls, old people, and children too![38]

*

The wolf lives with the lamb,
the panther lies down with the kid,
calf and lion cub feed together
with a little boy to lead them.
The cow and the bear make friends,
their young lie down together.
The lion eats straw like the ox.
The infant plays over the cobra's hole;
into the viper's lair
the young child puts his hand.
They do no hurt, no harm,
on all my holy mountain,
for the country is filled with the knowledge of God
as the waters swell the sea.[39]

*

Sons of Israel, listen to the word of the Lord,
for the Lord indicts the inhabitants of the country:
there is no fidelity, no tenderness,
no knowledge of God in the country,
only perjury and lies, slaughter, theft,
adultery and violence, murder after murder.
This is why the country is in mourning, and all who live in it pine away,
even the wild animals and the birds of heaven;
the fish of the sea themselves are perishing.[40]

*

BAHA'I

Briefly, it is not only their fellow human beings that the beloved of God must treat with mercy and compassion, rather must they show forth the utmost loving kindness to every living creature . . . The feelings are one and the same, whether ye inflict pain on man or on beast. [41]

*

Nature is God's Will and is its expression in and through the contingent world. [42]

*

This nature is subjected to an absolute organisation, to determined laws, to a complete order and to a finished design, from which it will never depart – to such a degree, indeed, that if you look carefully and with keen sight, from the smallest invisible atom up to such large bodies of the world of existence as the globe of the sun or the other great stars and luminous spheres, whether you regard their arrangement, their composition, their form or their movement, you will find that all are in the highest degree of organisation and are under one law from which they will never depart. [43]

*

All these endless beings which inhabit the world, whether man, animal, vegetable, mineral – whatever they may be – are surely, each one of them, composed of elements. There is no doubt that this perfection which is in all beings, is caused by the creation of God from the compositing elements, by their appropriate mingling and proportionate quantities, the mode of their composition, and the influence of other beings. For all beings are connected together like a chain, and reciprocal help, assistance, and influence belonging to the properties of things, are the causes of the existence, development and growth of created beings.[44]

*

In the physical realm of creation, all things are eaters and eaten: the plant drinketh in the mineral, the animal doth crop and swallow down the plant, man doth feed upon the animal, and the mineral devoureth the body of man. Physical bodies are transferred past one barrier after another, from one life to another, and all things are subject to transformation and change, save only the essence of existence itself – since it is constant and immutable, and upon it is founded the life of every species and kind, of every contingent reality throughout the whole of creation.[45]

*

When . . . thou dost contemplate the innermost essence of all things, and the individuality of each, thou wilt behold the signs of thy Lord's mercy in every created thing, and see the spreading rays of His Names and Attributes throughout all the realm of being . . . Then wilt thou observe that the universe is a scroll that discloseth His hidden secrets, which are preserved in the well-guarded Tablet. And not an atom of all the atoms in existence, not a creature from amongst the creatures but speaketh His praise and telleth of His attributes and names, revealeth the glory of His might and guideth to His oneness and His mercy . . .

And whensoever thou dost gaze upon creation all entire, and dost observe the very atoms thereof, thou wilt note that the rays of the Sun of Truth are shed upon all things and shining within them, and telling of that Day-Star's splendours, Its mysteries, and the spreading of Its lights. Look thou upon the trees, upon the blossoms and fruits, even upon the stones. Here too wilt thou behold the Sun's rays shed upon them, clearly visible within them, and manifested by them.[46]

*

SIKH

Rain has fallen, by the Lord it was poured down. All living creatures are allowed to dwell in comfort. The troubles are gone, comfort has set in, the true name of Hari, Hari, I will remember, O Lord! Whose they were, by him they were cherished. The Supreme Brahm has become (their) protector. By my Lord (their) supplication was heard, (their) calamity was brought to an end (by thee), O Lord! To all creatures he is giving. By the favour of the Guru he has looked down in mercy. In water, land and on the face of the earth all have been satiated; I will wash the feet of the holy one (the Guru), O Lord! The desire of the heart he is bringing about. I always, always sacrifice myself (for him). By the destroyer of pain a gift was given to Nanak; thou gratifiest those, who are imbued with love (to thee), O Lord![47]

*

God created the night, the seasons, days of the month and week.

He created the wind, water, fire and the worlds below.

In their midst he set the world as the sphere of dharma.

In it he placed animals of various species and colour,

Their names are many and endless.

Each one is judged according to his deeds.

The Lord Himself is True and His Court is true,

There the elect rejoice in their acceptance.

They bear the sign of grace and mercy.

There the bad and the good are separated.

Nanak, when we go there this will be manifest.

In the stage of Truth, the Formless One resides.

He, the Creator, beholds His creation and looks upon it with grace.

Here there are continents, worlds and universes.

Who can describe a boundless bound?

Here there are worlds within worlds and endless forms.

Whatever God wills, that they do freely.

God beholds His creation and rejoices. [48]

PRAYER
AND
PROSE

BUDDHISM

Come back, O Tigers! to the wood again,
And let it not be levelled with the plain;
For, without you, the axe will lay it low;
You, without it, for ever homeless go.[49]

*

May all beings everywhere
Plagued with sufferings of body and mind
Obtain an ocean of happiness and joy
By virtue of my merits.

May those feeble with cold find warmth.
And may those oppressed with heat be cooled
By the boundless waters that pour forth
From the great clouds of the Bodhisattvas (merits).

May the regions of desolation become places of joy
With vast and fragrant lotus pools
Beautified with the exquisite calls
Of wild ducks, geese and swans.

May the rains of lava, blazing stones and weapons
From now on become a rain of flowers.
And may all battling with weapons
From now on be a playful exchange of flowers.

May all animals be free from the fear
Of being eaten by one another;

May the hungry ghosts be as happy
As men of Lands of Plenty.

May the naked find clothing,
The hungry find food;
May the thirsty find water
and delicious drinks.

May the frightened cease to be afraid
and those bound be freed;
May the powerless find power;
and may people think of benefiting one another.

For as long as space endures
And for as long as living beings remain,
Until then may I too abide
To dispel the misery of the world.

May all the pains of living creatures
Ripen (solely) upon myself,
And through the might of the Bodhisattva Sangha
May all beings experience happiness.

May all embodied creatures
Uninterruptedly hear
The sound of Dharma issuing from birds and trees,
Beams of light and even space itself.

May there abound in all directions
Gardens of wish-fulfilling trees
Filled with the sweet sound of Dharma
Proclaimed by the Buddhas and the Bodhisattvas.[50]

*

Mind set free in the Dharma-realm,
I sit at the moon-filled window.
Watching the mountains with my ears,
Hearing the stream with open eyes.
Each molecule preaches perfect law,
Each moment chants true sutra:
The most fleeting thought is timeless,
A single hair's enough to stir the sea.[51]

*

It's not nature that upholds utility.
Look! even the rootless tree is swelled
With bloom, not red nor white, but lovely all the same.
How many can boast so fine a springtide?[52]

*

"Whether they belong to more evolved species like humans or to simpler ones such as animals, all beings primarily seek peace, comfort, and security. Life is as dear to the mute animal as it is to any human being; even the simplest insect strives for protection from dangers that threaten its life. Just as each one of us wants to live and does not wish to die, so it is wilt all other creatures in the universe, though their power to effect this is a different matter."[53]

CHRISTIANITY

Good Lord, most high almighty,
To you all praise is due,
All glory, honour, blessing,
Belong alone to you;
There is no man whose lips
Are fit to frame your name.

Be praised then, my Lord God,
In and through all your creatures,
Especially among them,
Through our Noble Brother Sun,
By whom you light our day;
In his radiant splendid beauty
He reminds us, Lord, of you.

Be praised, my Lord, through Sister Moon and all
    the stars;
You have made the sky shine in their lovely light.

In Brother Wind be praised, my Lord,
And in the air,
In clouds, in calm,
In all the weather moods that cherish life.

Be praised, my Lord, through Sister Water;
She is most useful, humble, precious, pure.
And Brother Fire, by whom you lighten night;
How fine is he, how happy, powerful, strong.

Through our dear Mother Earth be praised, my Lord,
She feeds us, guides us, gives us plants, bright flowers
And all her fruits.

Be praised, my Lord, through men
When out of love for you
We pardon one another.
When we endure
In sickness and in sorrow
Blessed are they who persevere in peace;
From you, Most High, they will receive their prize.

Be praised, my Lord, praised for our Sister Death,
From whom no man alive can hope to hide;
Wretched are they who die deep in their sin.
And blessed those, Death finds doing your will . . .
For them there is no further death to fear.

O Men! praise God and bless him,
Give him thanks
And serve him very humbly.[54]

*

"The animals and the wild beasts bend their knees and leave their byres and their lairs to raise their eyes to heaven, not without uttering sounds and making their breath heard in their own way. And the birds, now as they rise, turn towards heaven and form a cross with their wings like hands, saying something that seems like a prayer."[55]

*

"Our God has created nothing unnecessarily and has omitted nothing that is necessary."[56]

*

"The solicitude of storks for their old would be sufficient, if our children would reflect upon it, to make them love their parents; because there is no one so failing in good sense, as not to deem it a shame to be surpassed in virtue by birds devoid of reason. The storks surround

their father, when old age makes his feathers drop off, warm him with their wings, and provide abundantly for his support, and even in their flight they help him as much as they are able, raising him gently on each side upon their wings."[57]

*

"The Creator has submitted all to our rule, because we have been made in his image. It is not in great animals only that we see unapproachable wisdom; no less wonders are seen in the smallest. The high tops of the mountains which, near to the clouds and continually beaten by the winds, keep up a perpetual winter, do not arouse more admiration in me than the hollow valleys, which escape the storms of lofty peaks and preserve a constant mild temperature. In the same way in the constitution of animals I am no more astonished at the size of the elephant, than at the mouse, which is feared by the elephant, or at the scorpion's delicate sting, which has been hallowed like a pipe by the supreme artificer to throw venom into the wounds it makes. And let no one accuse the Creator of having produced venomous animals as destroyers and enemies of our life."[58]

*

"Earth has welcomed you with its own plants, water with its fish, air with its birds; the continent in its turn is ready to offer you its rich treasures . . . May he who has filled all with the works of his creation and has left everywhere visible memorials of his wonders, fill your hearts with all spiritual joys in Jesus Christ, our Lord, to whom belong glory and power, world without end. Amen."[59]

*

"In the sensible world itself, though there is a considerable mutual opposition of its various elements, yet a certain harmony maintained in those opposites has been devised by the wisdom that rules the universe, and thus there is produced a concord of the whole creation with itself, and the natural contrariety does not break the chain of agreement; in like manner, owing to the divine wisdom, there is an admixture and interpenetration of the sensible with the intellectual department, in order that all things may equally have a share in the beautiful, and no single one of existing things be without its share in that superior world."[60]

"Man was introduced into the world last after creation, not being thrown back to the end as contemptible, but as one who was called to control that which was made subject to him at his very birth . . . God places in him the principles of a double creation, having mingled the divine with the earthly, that by means of both he may be naturally and properly disposed to each enjoyment, enjoying God by means of his more divine nature, and the good things of the earth by the sense that is akin to them."[61]

*

"He [God] placed him on the earth, a new angel, a mingled worshipper, fully initiated into the visible creation, but only partially into the intellectual; King of all upon the earth, but subject to the King above; earthly and heavenly; temporal and yet immortal; visible and yet intellectual; halfway between greatness and lowliness; in one person combining spirit and flesh."[62]

*

"It would be ridiculous . . . to regard the defects of beasts, trees and other mutable and mortal things . . . as deserving of condemnation. Such defects do indeed effect the decay of their nature, which is liable to dissolution; but these creatures have received their mode of being by the will of their Creator, whose purpose is that they should bring to perfection the beauty of the lower parts of the universe by their alteration and succession in the passage of the seasons; and this is a beauty in its own kind, finding its place among the constituent parts of the world . . . Therefore it is the nature of things considered in itself, without regard to our convenience or inconvenience, that gives glory to the Creator . . . And so all nature's substances are good, because they exist and therefore have their own mode and kind of being, and, in their fashion, a peace and harmony among themselves."[63]

"I spoke to all the things that were about me, all that can be admitted by the door of the senses, 'Since you are not my God, tell me about him. Tell me something of my God.' Clear and loud they answered me, 'God is he who made us.' I asked these questions simply by gazing at these things, and their beauty was all the answer they gave me".[64]

*

Therefore, open your eyes,
alert the ears of your spirit, open your lips
and apply your heart
so that in all creatures you may
see, hear, praise, love and worship, glorify and honour your God
lest the whole world rise against you.
For because of this
the whole world will fight against the foolish.
On the contrary,
it will be a matter of glory for the wise,
who can say with the Prophet:
You have gladdened me, Lord, by your deeds
and in the works of your hands I will rejoice.
How great are your works, Lord!
You have made all things in wisdom;
the earth is filled with your creatures.[65]

*

For this I thank You, that You have created me to Your image, and placed Your wonders under my hands so that I may know them and rejoice in the works of Your creation.

I pray to You, eternal God, give me understanding and wisdom that I might not misuse Your creation but use it only for my needs, for the good of my neighbour, myself (and my family). Give me gratitude for all Your gifts, so that my reason does not say: 'This is mine. I have purchased it. I will possess it alone. I am noble with it, majestic and beautiful; it belongs to me because of this honour and glory.' All this comes from the devil and the grievous fall of Adam.[66]

Now the preaching of St Francis was on this wise: "My sisters the birds, much are ye beholden unto God your creator, and always and in every place ought ye to praise Him, because He hath given you liberty to fly wheresoever ye will, and hath clothed you on with twofold and threefold raiment. Moreover, He preserved your seed in the ark of Noah that your race might not be destroyed. Again, ye are beholden unto Him for the element of the air which He hath appointed for you; furthermore, ye sow not neither do ye reap; yet God feedeth you and giveth you rivers and fountains wherefrom to drink; He giveth you mountains and valleys for your refuge, and high trees wherein to build your nests; and, in that ye know not how to sew nor spin, God clotheth you and your little ones; wherefore doth your Creator love you seeing that He giveth you so many benefits.

Guard yourselves, therefore, my sisters the birds, from the sin of ingratitude and be ye ever mindful to give praise to God."[67]

*

HINDUISM

One should treat animals such as deer, camels, asses, monkeys, mice, snakes, birds and flies exactly like one's own son. How little difference there actually is between children and these innocent animals.[68]

*

Everything animate or inanimate that is within the universe is controlled and owned by the Lord. One should therefore accept only those things necessary for himself, which are set aside as his quota, and one should not accept other things, knowing well to whom they belong.[69]

*

My footsteps
I know you hear night and day.
Your pleasure
Blooms in the purple of autumn's dawn,
Sparkles in the springtime shower of blossoms.
The nearer I come to you on your path,
The livelier dances the sea.
Like lotus-petals my life unfolds
From birth to birth,
And your crowding suns and stars
Circle men in wonder.
The blossom of the world woven of light

Fills your offering hands,
And your shy heaven
Unfolds its love,
Petal by petal,
In my sky.

To the bird you have given song,
Therefore it sings;
To me you have given only a voice,
But I give back more –
I sing.

The wind you have made free,
Therefore it lightly obeys your commands;
But me you have loaded with burdens,
With them I toil on.
Passing from death to death,
Slowly I free myself from them,
Till empty-handed I come
Ready to serve you.

the full-moon you have endowed with a smile,
It pours forth its loveliness
And fills with beauty the cup of earth.
My brow which you have touched with sorrow,
I wash with tears, transforming it into joy.
Mingling darkness with light
Have you created your earth;
To that earth you send me
Empty-handed.
Watching me with a smile hidden behind your void,
You command me to transform it into heaven.

To all you give,
Only from me do you demand.
Descending from your throne,
Smilingly you take to your heart
What out of love I offer you.
What you lay in my hands,
A thousand times enriched
It returns to you.[70]

*

You are the forest

you are all the great trees
in the forest

you are bird and beast
playing in and out
of all the trees

O lord white as jasmine
filling and filled by all

why don't you
show me your face?

Would a circling surface vulture
know such depths of sky
as the moon would know?

Would a weed in the riverbank
know such depths of water
as the lotus would know?

Would a fly darting nearby
know the smell of flowers
as the bee would know?

O lord white as jasmine
only you would know
the way of your devotees:
how would these,

these
mosquitos
on the buffalo's hide?[71]

*

Ahimsa is a comprehensive principle. We are helpless mortals caught in the conflagration of himsa. The saying that life lives on life has a deep meaning in it. Man cannot for a moment live without consciously or unconsciously committing outward himsa. The very fact of his living – eating, drinking and moving about – necessarily involves some himsa, destruction of life, be it ever so minute. A votary of ahimsa therefore remains true to his faith if the spring of all his actions is compassion, if he shuns to the best of his ability the destruction of the tiniest creature, tries to save it, and thus incessantly strives to be free from the deadly coil of himsa.[72]

*

ISLAM

Abu Hurairah said:
The Messenger of Allah (peace and blessings of Allah be on him) said: "A prostitute was forgiven – she passed by a dog, panting with its tongue out, on the top of a well containing water, almost dying with thirst; so she took off her boot and tied it to her head-covering and drew forth water for it; she was forgiven on account of this."

It was said: Is there a reward for us in (doing good to) the beasts? He said: "In every animal having a liver fresh with life there is a reward."

Doing good to beasts is like the doing of good to human beings, a deed of charity; while cruelty to animals is forbidden just like cruelty to human beings.[73]

*

Know that the world is a mirror from head to foot,
In every atom are a hundred blazing suns.
If you cleave the heart of one drop of water,
A hundred pure oceans emerge from it.
If you examine closely each grain of sand,
A thousand Adams may be seen in it.
In its members a gnat is like an elephant,
In its qualities a drop of rain is like the Nile.
The heart of a piece of corn equals a hundred harvests,

A world dwells in the heart of a millet seed.
In the wing of a gnat is the ocean of life.
In the pupil of the eye a heaven.
What though the corn grain of the heart be small
It is a station of the Lord of both worlds of dwell
*   therein.*[74]

*

Praise to the Holy Creator, who has placed his throne upon the waters, and who has made all terrestrial creatures. To the Heavens he has given dominion and to the Earth dependence; to the Heavens he has given movement, and to the Earth uniform repose.

He raised the firmament above the earth as a tent, without pillars to uphold it. In six days he created the seven planets and with two letters he created the nine cupolas of the Heavens.

In the beginning he gilded the stars, so that at night the heavens might play tric-trac.

With diverse properties he endowed the net of the body, and he has put dust on the tail of the bird of the soul.

He made the Ocean liquid as a sign of bondage, and the mountain tops are capped with ice for fear of him.

He dried up the bed of the sea and from its stones brought forth rubies, and from its blood, musk.

To the mountains he has given peaks for a dagger, and valleys for a belt; so that they lift up their heads in pride.

Sometimes he makes clusters of roses spring from the face of the fire;

Sometimes he throws bridges across the face of the waters.

He caused a mosquito to sting Nimrod his enemy who thereby suffered for four hundred years.

In his wisdom he caused the spider to spin his web to protect the highest of men.

He squeezed the waist of the ant so that it resembled a hair, and he made it a companion of Solomon;

He gave it the black robes of the Abbasides

and a garment of unwoven brocade worthy of the peacock.

When he saw that the carpet of nature was defective he pieced it together fittingly. [75]

*

Created beings are the dependents of Allah, so the creature dearest to Allah is he who does most good to Allah's dependants. [76]

Whoever revives dead land, for him is reward in it; and whatever any creature seeking food eats of it, shall be reckoned as charity from him. [77]

*

There is no Muslim who plants a tree or sows a field and a human, bird or animal eats from it, but it shall be reckoned as charity from him. [78]

JEWISH

"Listen", replied Rabbi Yitzchak. "A traveller was once journeying through the desert, and when weary, hungry, and thirsty, he happened upon an oasis, where grew a fruitful tree, wide-branched, and at the foot of which there gushed a spring of clear, cool water.

The stranger ate of the luscious fruit, enjoying and resting in the grateful shade, and quenching his thirst in the sparkling water which bubbled merrily at his feet.

When about to resume his journey, he addressed the tree and spoke as follows:

'Oh, gracious tree, with what words can I bless thee, and what good can I wish thee? I cannot wish thee good fruit, for it is already thine; the blessing of water is also thine, and the gracious shade thrown by the beauteous branches the Eternal has already granted thee, for my good and the good of those who travel by this way. Let me pray to God, then, that all thy offspring may be goodly as thyself.'

So it is with thee, my pupil. How shall I bless thee? Thou art perfect in the law, eminent in the land, respected, and blessed with means. May God grant that all thy offspring may prove goodly as thyself." [79]

*

I look up to the sky and its stars,
And down to the earth and the things that creep there.
And I consider in my heart how their creation
Was planned with wisdom in every detail.
See the heavens above like a tent,
Constructed with loops and with hooks,
And the moon with its stars, like a shepherdess
Driving her sheep to pasture;
The moon itself among the clouds,
Like a ship sailing under its banners;
The clouds like a girl in her garden
Moving, and watering the myrtle-trees;
The dew-mist – a woman shaking
Drops from her hair on the ground.
The inhabitants turn, like animals, to rest,
(Their palaces like their stables);
And all fleeing from the fear of death,
Like a dove pursued by the falcon.
And these are compared at the end to a plate
Which is smashed into innumerable sherds. [80]

*

Who established the heavens on high? Who stretched
out the sphere of the stars?
Which god is great like God? Who can speak of the
divine powers?
Before you, O god, praise is dumb.

Who spoke and his word prevailed, when he spread
out his skies?
Who ordered and his order stood, when he disposed his
world?
Who put boundaries round the seas, when he
determined their lines?
Who joined the clods of the earth, when he constructed
its valleys?
Who fixed the earth's dimensions? Do you know?
Who held the rule?

Who puts on a robe of glory, and wraps himself in
honour?
In whose memory is righteousness, whose ways are
humility?
Who is the powerful God, full of strength, before
whom the lofty bow?

Who utters mysteries, and proclaims them by word of
mouth?
Who speaks and it happens, without the Lord's
command?

Who threw the breakers into the depths of the sea?
Who spaced each wave at three hundred leagues?
Who uttered a word to pierce a channel for the rain?
Who brought each drop from its own mould to
promote fertility? [81]

*

Rabbi Schneur Zalman taught: Everyone who has insight into the matter will understand clearly that everything created and having being is as absolute naught with regard to the Activating Force, which is in all created being. This Force constitutes its reality and draws it forth from absolute nothingness to being. The fact that all created things seem to have existence and being in their own right is because we can neither conceive nor see with our physical eyes, the Force of God which is in the created world. Were the eye able to see and conceive the vitality and spirituality in each created thing, which flows through it from its divine source, then the physicality, materiality and substantiality of the created world would not be seen at all; because apart from the spiritual dimension it is absolute nothingness. There is really nothing in existence besides God. [82]

*

When the Holy One – blessed be He! – created the world, it was a level expanse free from mountains; but when Cain slew Abel his brother, whose blood was trodden down on the earth, He cursed the ground, and immediately hills and mountains sprang into existence. [83]

*

Adam walked in the Garden on the first day. He smelled wonderful scents and enjoyed the beautiful sight. The aroma of the ripened fruit drew him to the trees. He reached for an apricot that hung from a branch. The fruit lifted itself so that he could not touch it. He reached for a pomegranate. The fruit evaded his hand. Then a voice spoke, "Till the soil and care for the trees and then you may eat."[84]

A wise rabbi was walking along a road when he saw a man planting a tree. The rabbi asked him, "How many years will it take for this tree to bear fruit?" The man answered that it would take seventy years. The rabbi asked, "Are you so fit and strong that you expect to live that long and eat its fruit?" The man answered, "I found a fruitful world because my forefathers planted for me. So I will do the same for my children."[85]

CHINESE

The Tao flows to all places, both to the left and the right. All creatures depend upon it for life, yet it claims no authority over creation. It does what is needed to sustain life but seeks no glory. All creatures are fed and clothed by it yet it is not their master. Small in ambition or desire, when all creatures turn to it, although not their master, yet it is truly great. Being without display, it is indeed great.[86]

*

The trees on the Ox Mountain were once beautiful. However, because the mountain is on the borders of a great state, they were cut down with axes and saws, so how could they retain their beauty? Yet they continued through the cycle of life and the feeding of the rain and dew to put forth buds and new leaves. But the cattle and goats came and browsed amongst the trees and destroyed them. This is why the mountain is now bare and stripped. People look at it and think this is how it has always been. But this is not the true nature of the mountain.

And this is also the case with humanity. Surely we were not without benevolence and righteousness? The way in which a person loses their true goodness is just like the way trees are destroyed by the axe. Cut down day after day, how can the mind, anymore than the tree, retain its beauty or continue to live?[87]

*

In the ancient days when proper natural behaviour was still possible, people moved quietly and saw clearly. In those days there were no roadways across the mountains; no boats or bridges crossing the rivers. All things were created each for its own true sphere. The birds and beasts multiplied while the trees and bushes flourished. Birds could be held in the hand – it was possible to look into the nest of the raven. In those days we lived with all birds and animals and all of the creation was as one. Nor were there any good or bad people for as everyone was without knowledge, no-one could be led astray. As everyone was without evil so all were in a state of harmony with nature, the true perfection of being human.[88]

*

Light is born of darkness. Classification is born of formlessness. The Soul is born of Tao. The body is born of vital essence. Thus all things produce after their kind. Creatures with nine channels of communication are born from the womb. Creatures with eight are born from the egg. Of their coming there is no trace. In their departure there is no goal. No entrance gate, no dwelling house, they pass this way and that, as though at the meeting of crossroads . . .

Heaven cannot but be high. Earth cannot but be broad. The sun and moon cannot but revolve. All creation cannot but flourish. To do so is their Tao.[89]

*

51

PILGRIMAGE
FOR
LIFE

IT DIDN'T seem to matter whether they walked in brilliant sunshine, or were buffeted by the winds and rains which came rolling down from the Umbrian hills. On they came, with banners unfurled, wearing the distinctive sun-and-moon tabards, like some crusader army. The sound of many tongues and the clamour of spontaneous singing rang out as they walked from village to village. At each stop, the message was passed on and shared with villagers, townspeople and the tourists. The message was simple. "We believe in conservation." Some believed because they were conservationists, who had studied the impact of humanity on the environment and knew only too well how great is the crisis of our physical world. Others were walking because of the beliefs which their faith gave them. Christians, following the example of St Francis, whose love for all life earned him the name 'the second Christ'. Muslims, exploring the consequences of our being the viceregents of God. Hindus, drawing upon the profound reverence for life which lies at the core of that faith. Buddhists, walking in the path of the Compassionate One. A Maori Elder, bringing testimony of the wisdom contained in the traditional cultures of the world. Zoroastrians, Jains, Sikhs, Baha'is and many others, all walking side by side because of what they believe about nature.

They were coming by stages to the Umbrian hilltown of Assisi at the invitation of a most unlikely host. For the World Wide Fund for Nature International (WWF) had decided that for its 25th Anniversary it would invite the great faiths of the world to come on pilgrimage to Assisi in order to hear what religion had to offer to conservation and what conservation had to share with religion.

And come they did, from all parts of the world. As well as pilgrims, there were senior religious leaders empowered by their organisations to speak authoritatively for the faith. There were musicians and dancers, singers and actors sharing through their arts the insights to be found in the religious traditions of the world about nature. There were leading conservationists representing the many national organisations of the WWF as well as a host of other conservation bodies. It was the most extraordinary gathering for conservation ever seen, and many who came were unsure how it would work. For here were worlds which had been separate or at least distant for so long. There were the problems of different faiths coming together yet retaining their integrity. There was the difficulty of reconciling the worlds of science and faith which for so many and for so long have seemed to be irreconcilable. Yet something greater than all these divisions drew them to Assisi, for better or for worse: concern that the natural world could well collapse and die unless ways forward were found.

The pilgrimages acted as the main symbol of the Event. By coming on foot to Assisi, the pilgrims reminded all they met or all who heard of them (for the world's media followed the events with a keen interest) of the need to walk humbly and to walk carefully, yet also to rejoice and to celebrate. There were four routes, two roughly from the north of Assisi coming from the towns of Cortona and Gubbio, and two from the south from Nocera Umbra and Spoleto. Hospitality had been jointly arranged by the WWF Italy volunteers and staff and the Franciscans. Food was provided by nuns, town councils, priests, teachers and their schools and by ordinary citizens. Accommodation was likewise drawn from a wide range of supporters wherever the pilgrimages stayed. And in the evenings, both to thank their hosts and to celebrate the challenge and promise of difference and diversity, there were performances from some of the world's leading artists in particular cultures.

On the first night of the Cortona pilgrimage, the ancient town witnessed a vast puppet, over 12 feet tall, striding through the streets. This was the Mother of Sorrows, Mother Mary and Mother Earth rolled into one in a dramatic new version of the Mystery and Passion plays of medieval Christianity by actors from England. Three nights later, the town of Umbertide came alive to Sudanese, Muslim nomadic dance and music. Abdul and his team of musicians drew the entire audience to its feet and soon the town square was a mass of people dancing to the haunting rhythms of nomadic song. On another night, Tim Wheater, a Baha'i and master flautist wandered by accident into the wrong inn in a small village. Thinking to find the pilgrims he accidentally stumbled upon the local football team and supporters celebrating a crushing victory over their local rivals. Tim realised all might not be right when the act before him turned out to be three scantily clad young ladies who finished their act with even less on than when they began. Feeling a little like a fish out of water, Tim stepped forward and began to play.

Eventually the noise of the applause and the sound of the music drew the waiting pilgrims to the spot, where they had to battle to get near, so great was the crush of villagers. Tim was eventually allowed to stop sometime near dawn.

Meanwhile in Assisi representatives of the five major faiths, Buddhism, Christianity, Hinduism, Islam and Judaism, met in retreat. The Convent of the Basilica of St Francis was their home throughout the Event. Here the five faiths shared their insights and beliefs, hopes and fears for nature and as part of nature.

On Sunday 28th September, the three streams flowing to create the final Event of Assisi met. The pilgrims marched into Assisi, flags flying, through the north and south gates. Here they were greeted in a glorious cacophony of sound and colour by the religious performers, Hungarian Jewish singers; Zambian Catholic singers; Tibetan horns and dancers and so on. Now surging through the streets of Assisi, the joyful procession passed on until it came to the top of the hill leading down to the basilica. Waiting for the pilgrims and performers were the religious representatives and HRH Prince Philip, International president of the WWF. This event had been his idea in the first place. He read a book written for the WWF UK by Martin Palmer and Esther Bissett called "Worlds of Difference". This book, designed for schools, looked at how eight different belief systems viewed nature as a result of their creation stories, and how this affected the way people live. From this had sprung the chain of events which now led to Prince Philip standing side by side with religious leaders while the pilgrim band swept down the hill towards them.

Soon the great piazza in front of the basilica was full of people and the air was filled with streamers, balloons and noise while the pilgrims were greeted by the religious representatives and HRH Prince Philip.

The following day, the drama of Assisi came to a climax.

No one present in the Basilica of St Francis of Assisi on 29th September, 1986, will ever forget the experience. 800 people participated in an inspiring and richly symbolic ceremony that brought together representatives of five great religions, the WWF family, pilgrims and guests, all to dedicate themselves to guarding the integrity of Creation.

All those present and, it is hoped, millions of people who were not present will also be influenced by this unprecedented event, for as WWF International's President, HRH The Duke of Edinburgh, announced during the ceremony, "a new and powerful alliance has been forged between the forces of religion and the forces of conservation."

An Italian journalist later wrote that "Giotto's frescoes of the life of St Francis had to wait more than 500 years to witness Buddhist, Hindu, Islamic and Jewish rituals within the nave of the church where the Roman Catholic patron saint of ecology lies buried. Nothing remotely like this has happened before."

It began with the voice of a muezzin high in a bell tower, as from a minaret, calling in Arabic for men to "ponder the creation of the heavens and the earth, and say; "Our Lord: you have not created this for nothing. Yours is the Glory'."

As the procession moved towards the Basilica doors, alp horns from WWF International's 'home' country, Switzerland, sounded an invitation. It was echoed in symbolic acceptance by Tibetan mountain horns. Suddenly a Maori warrior-priest from New Zealand halted Prince Philip with a challenge on behalf of the world's indigenous peoples to respect their perspectives of nature. Acceptance of the challenge was sealed in the Maori way as the two touched noses to the delight of the crowd gathered on the slope outside the church. Then the procession, followed by pilgrims bearing banners they had carried on foot to Assisi, entered the Basilica to Psalm 148 praising God the Creator sung by the Franciscan choir to a new setting by the British composer Ilona Sekacz.

Father Lanfranco Serrini, Minister General of the Franciscan Order, welcomed his unique congregation saying, "No one pretends that our respective beliefs are or can be held in common; but we do believe that religious concern for the conservation and ecological harmony of the natural world is our common heritage, our birthright and our duty . . . Let us now, each according to the wealth of our own religious traditions, celebrate our common concern for the future of the world."

The ceremony unfolded with five symbolic rituals drawn from each religion.

Thanksgiving for creation was symbolised by a renowned temple dancer from India, Yamini Krishnamurti, who whirled and gestured in colourful silks and tinkling anklets to enact a Hindu dance based on the creation Veda. Repentance was urged by Rabbi Arthur Hertzberg calling in all four directions from the Basilica entrance for contrition for our failure to care for nature, as the ram's horn shofar was blown. This call to repentance was repeated in the words of each religion – by the deep and thrilling chant of a prayer by His Holiness the Dalai Lama performed by three Tibetan monks, by Dr Karan Singh's reading from the Bhagavad-Gita, by Dr Abdullah Omar Nasseef's citation of the Qur'an and by Father Serrini's reading from the New Testament. A Kyrie Eleison by the Franciscan choir closed this section.

With celebratory prayers sung, chanted and read, banners for each of the five religions and WWF were ranged in the centre of the nave to symbolise the hope for the future of creation offered by the visions of each faith. The Duke of Edinburgh introduced this section hailing the new alliance and asking all to listen with open minds to the teachings of the great religions concerning the environment and the part that humanity should be playing in its protection.

The final act of Assisi was the issuing of the Declarations – the first act in the invitation to make what happened at Assisi part of the future, not just an interesting event of the past. For the first time ever, we have categorical and authoritative statements from within the five major faiths, stating as simply as possible where they stand on the issue of ecology and of nature. These Declarations speak in the language, symbolism and vitality of each particular faith. There was no 'final statement' from Assisi claiming uniformity. For each faith is different and distinct and it is the distinctive insights which we all need, not some superficial unity which removes that which makes people hold to their faith and motivates their actions. With these clear calls to care for nature or to recognise our oneness with nature, the religions have placed themselves firmly into the world of active as well as thoughtful conservation, but on their own terms. Likewise conservation can now reach out through these faiths to touch people for whom the secular versions of conservation have little to say or offer.

THE
BUDDHIST
DECLARATION
ON
NATURE

THERE is a natural relationship between a cause and its resulting consequences in the physical world. In the life of the sentient beings too, including animals, there is a similar relationship of positive causes bringing about happiness and negative actions causing negative consequences. Therefore, a human undertaking motivated by a healthy and positive attitude constitutes one of the most important causes of the happiness, while undertakings generated through ignorance and negative attitude bring about suffering and misery. And this positive human attitude is, in the final analysis, rooted in genuine and unselfish compassion and loving kindness that seeks to bring about light and happiness for all sentient beings. Hence Buddhism is a religion of love, understanding and compassion, and committed towards the ideal of non-violence. As such, it also attaches great importance to wild life and the protection of the environment on which every being in this world depends for survival.

*

Many additional factors contribute to and reinforce this insight in Buddhism. A philosophical system which propagates the theory of rebirth and life after death, it maintains that in the continuous birth and rebirth of sentient beings (not only on this planet but in the universe as a whole) each being is related to us ourselves, just as our own parents are related to us in this life.

*

We are told that history is a record of human society in the past. From existing sources there is evidence to suggest that for all their limitations, people in the past were aware of this need for harmony between human beings and nature. They loved the environment. They revered it as the source of life and wellbeing in the world. In my faraway country, I still remember what my parents said: they told us that various spirits and forces are dormant in the rivers, mountains, lakes and trees. Any harm done to them, they said, would result in drought, epidemics and sickness in human beings, and the loss of the fertility of the earth.

We regard our survival as an undeniable right. As co-inhabitants of this planet, other species too have this right for survival. And since human beings as well as other non-human sentient beings depend upon the environment as the ultimate source of life and wellbeing, let us share the conviction that the conservation of the environment, the restoration of the imbalance caused by our negligence in the past, be implemented with courage and determination.

These teachings lead us to the following words by His Holiness the Dalai Lama:
"Various crises face the international community. The mass starvation of human beings and the extinction of species may not have overshadowed the great achievements in science and technology, but they have assumed equal proportions. Side by side with the exploration of outer space, there is the continuing pollution of lakes, rivers and vast parts of the oceans, out of human ignorance and misunderstanding. There is a great danger that future generations will not know the natural habitat of animals; they may not know the forests and the animals which we of this generation know to be in danger of extinction.

We are the generation with the awareness of a great danger. We are the ones with the responsibility and the ability to take steps of concrete action, before it is too late."

*

THE CHRISTIAN DECLARATION ON NATURE

GOD declared everything to be good, indeed, very good. He created nothing unnecessarily and has omitted nothing that is necessary. Thus, even in the mutual opposition of the various elements of the universe, there exists a divinely willed harmony because creatures have received their mode of existence by the will of their Creator, whose purpose is that through their interdependence they should bring to perfection the beauty of the universe. It is the very nature of things considered in itself, without regard to man's convenience or inconvenience, that gives glory to the Creator.

*

The Fathers of the Church understood well the marvel of man's dual citizenship and the responsibilities it placed upon him. In the words of St Gregory of Nazianzen, "God sees man upon earth as a kind of second world, a microcosm; another kind of angel, a worshipper of blended nature . . . He was kind of all upon earth, but subject to heaven; earthly and heavenly; transient, yet immortal; belonging both to the visible and to the intelligible order; midway between greatness and lowliness."

*

Most certainly then, because of the responsibilities which flow from his dual citizenship, man's dominion cannot be understood as licence to abuse, spoil, squander or destroy what God has made to manifest his glory. That dominion cannot be anything other than a stewardship in symbiosis with all creatures. On the one hand, man's position verges on a viceregal partnership with God; on the other, his self-mastery in symbiosis with creation must manifest the Lord's exclusive and absolute dominion over everything, over man and over his stewardship. At the risk of destroying himself, man may not reduce to chaos or disorder, or, worse still, destroy God's bountiful treasures.

Every human act of irresponsibility towards creatures is an abomination. According to its gravity, it is an offence against that divine wisdom which sustains and gives purpose to the interdependent harmony of the universe.

*

Since God can express his will through all of his works, Francis was submissive to all creatures and scanned creation attentively, listening to its mysterious voices. In his 'Canticle of Brother Sun' the saint called all creatures his brothers and sisters because they are God's gifts and signs of his providential and reconciling love. To God alone do they belong, to him they bear a likeness, and in his name Mother Earth, our sister, feeds us. In his personalized relationship with all creatures. St Francis recognized his duty to reciprocate divine love with love and praise, not only in the name of creatures, but in, with and through them.

THE HINDU DECLARATION ON NATURE

In the ancient spiritual traditions, man was looked upon as part of nature, linked by indissoluble spiritual and psychological bonds with the elements around him. This is very much marked in the Hindu tradition, probably the oldest living religions tradition in the world.

*

Hinduism believes in the all encompassing sovereignty of the divine, manifesting itself in a graded scale of evolution. The human race, though at the top of the evolutionary pyramid at present, is not seen as something apart from the earth and its multitudinous lifeforms. The Atharva Veda has the magnificent Hymn to the Earth which is redolent with ecological and environmental values.

*

The Hindu viewpoint on nature is permeated by a reverence for life, and an awareness that the great forces of nature – the earth, the sky, the air, the water and fire – as well as various orders of life including plants, and trees, forests and animals, are all bound to each other within the great rhythms of nature. The divine is not exterior to creation, but expresses itself through natural phenomena.

*

Apart from this, the natural environment also received the close attention of the ancient Hindu scriptures. Forests and groves were considered sacred, and flowering trees received special reverence. Just as various animals were associated with gods and goddesses, different trees and plants were also associated in the Hindu pantheon. The Mahabharata says that "even if there is only one tree full of flowers and fruits in a village, that place becomes worthy of worship and respect." Various trees, fruits and plants have special significance in Hindu rituals.

The Hindu tradition of reverence for nature and all forms of life, vegetable or animal, represents a powerful tradition which needs to be re-nurtured and re-applied in our contemporary context.

*

This earth, so touchingly looked upon in the Hindu view as the Universal Mother, has nurtured mankind up from the slime of the primeval ocean for billions of years. Let us declare our determination to halt the present slide towards destruction, to rediscover the ancient tradition of reverence for all life and, even at this late hour, to reverse the suicidal course upon which we have embarked. Let us recall the ancient Hindu dictum: "The Earth is our mother, and we are all her children."

*

THE ISLAMIC DECLARATION ON NATURE

THE essence of Islamic teaching is that the entire universe is God's creation. Allah makes the waters flow upon the earth, upholds the heaven, makes the rain fall and keeps the boundaries between day and night. The whole of the rich and wonderful universe belongs to God, its maker. It is God who created the plants and the animals in their pairs and gave them the means to multiply. Then God created mankind – a very special creation because mankind alone was created with reason and the power to think and even the means to turn against his Creator. Mankind has the potential to acquire a status higher than that of the angels or sink lower than the lowliest of the beasts.

*

When we submit to the Will of God, we become aware of the sublime fact that all our powers, potentials, skills and knowledge are granted to us by God. We are His servants and when we are conscious of that, when we realise that all our achievements derive from the Mercy of God, when we return proper thanks and respect and worship to God for our nature and creation, then we become free. Our freedom is that of being sensible, aware, responsible trustees of God's gifts and bounty.

For the Muslim, mankind's role on earth is that of a 'khalifa', viceregent or trustee of God. We are God's stewards and agents on Earth. We are not masters of this Earth, it does not belong to us to do what we wish. It belongs to God and He has entrusted us with its safekeeping. Our function as viceregents, 'khalifa' of God, is only to oversee the trust. The 'khalifa' is answerable for his/her actions, for the way in which he/she uses or abuses the trust of God.

Allah is Unity; and His Unity is also reflected in the unity of mankind, and the unity of man and nature. His trustees are responsible for maintaining the unity of His creation, the integrity of the Earth, its flora and fauna, its wildlife and natural environment. Unity cannot be had by discord, by setting one need against another or letting one end predominate over another; it is maintained by balance and harmony.

*

So unity, trusteeship and accountability, that is 'tawheed', 'khalifa' and 'akhrah', the three central concepts of Islam, are also the pillars of the environmental ethics of Islam. They constitute the basic values taught by the Qur'an. It is these values which led Muhammad, the Prophet of Islam, to say: "whoever plants a tree and diligently looks after it until it matures and bears fruit is rewarded", and "If a Muslim plants a tree or sows a field and men and beasts and birds eat from it, all of it is charity on his part", and again, "The world is green and beautiful and God has appointed you his stewards over it." Environmental consciousness is born when such values are adopted and become an intrinsic part of our mental and physical make-up.

*

THE JEWISH DECLARATION ON NATURE

W HEN God created the world, so the Bible tells us, He made order out of primal chaos. The sun, the moon, and the stars, plants, animals, and ultimately man, were each created with a rightful and necessary place in the universe. They were not to encroach on each other. "Even the divine teaching, the Torah, which was revealed from on high, was given in a set measure" (Vayikra Rabbah 15:2) and even these holy words may not extend beyond their assigned limit.

"And the Lord took man and put him in the Garden of Eden, to tend it and guard it" (Genesis 2:15). Soon Adam, man, the one creature who is most godlike, gave names to all of creation, as God looked on and approved. "And the name that Adam gave to each living being has remained its name." (Genesis 2:19) forever. In the Kabbalistic teaching, as Adam named all of God's creatures, he helped define their essence. Adam swore to live in harmony with those whom he had named. Thus, at the very beginning of time, man accepted responsibility before God for all of creation.

*

The highest form of obedience to God's commandments is to do them not in mere acceptance but in the nature of union with Him. In such a joyous encounter between man and God, the very rightness of the world is affirmed. The encounter of God and man in nature is thus conceived in Judaism as a seamless web with man as the leader and custodian of the natural world.

*

There is a tension at the centre of the Biblical tradition, embedded in the very story of creation itself, over the question of power and stewardship. The world was created because God willed it, but why did He will it? Judaism has maintained, in all of its versions, that this world is the arena that God created for man, half beast and half angel, to prove that he could behave as a moral being. The Bible did not fail to demand even of God Himself that He be bound, as much as man, by the law of morality. . . . Comparably, man was given dominion over nature, but he was commanded to behave towards the rest of creation with justice and compassion. Man lives, always, in tension between his power and the limits set by conscience.

Some twenty centuries ago they told the story of two men who were out on the water in a rowboat. Suddenly, one of them started to saw under his feet. He maintained that it was his right to do whatever he wished with the place which belonged to him. The other answered him that they were in the rowboat together; the hole that he was making would sink both of them. (Vayikra Rabbah 4:6).

We have a responsibility to life, to defend it everywhere, not only against our own sins but also against those of others. We are all passengers together in this same fragile and glorious world. Let us safeguard our rowboat – and let us row together.

*

These are selections from the "Assisi Declarations".

ASSISI
CEREMONY

WELCOME

W<small>E</small>, members of major world religions and traditions, and men and women of good will, are gathered here, in this marvellous Church of St Francis, to awaken all people to their historical responsibility for the welfare of Planet Earth, our Sister and Mother, who in her generous sovereignty feeds us and all her creatures.

Every major religion and tradition of the world is represented here. No one pretends that our respective beliefs are or can be held in common; but we do believe that religious concern for the conservation and ecological harmony of the natural world is our common heritage, our birthright and our duty.

*

Each religion will celebrate the dignity of nature and the duty of every person to live harmoniously within the natural world. We are convinced of the inestimable value of our respective traditions and of what they can offer to re-establish ecological harmony; but, at the same time, we are humble enough to desire to learn from each other. The very richness of our diversity lends strength to our shared concern and responsibility for our Planet Earth.

FATHER SERRINI OFM CONV.

CELEBRATION SECTION

We realise that we have got to come to terms with the fact that the dominance which human kind has acquired over the rest of the living world brings with it a direct responsibility for ensuring the survival of our fellow creatures and all forms of life on earth. This means that we have an obligation to halt the present headlong rush to destruction before it is too late.

The time has now come for us to look to the future, but before we can go forward we must, each in our own way, make an effort to understand the purpose of life and to rediscover what the prophets and visionaries had to say about Creation and about our relationship with the world about us.

*

We need vision to help us to see our responsibilities more clearly and to give us the inspiration and commitment to initiate and to carry through the measures to achieve a healthy and dynamic balance with nature. We need vision to help us to accept the inevitable sacrifices that these measures will entail. We need vision because, while it is easy enough to devise plans, we must have that sense of dedication that comes only from total conviction.

Vision also brings hope; hope that we can begin to halt and eventually to reverse the destruction of nature which we can so clearly see all around us. As the writer of the Book of Proverbs put it, 'Where there is no vision, the people perish.' I want to suggest that where there is no vision, all life will perish.

HRH THE DUKE OF EDINBURGH

The Venerable Lungrig Namgyal led the Buddhist monks in chanting verses from Shantideva's Guide to the Bodhisattva's Way of Life, which is reproduced in Section 2 of this book.

"As no-one desires the slightest suffering
Nor ever has enough of happiness,
There is no difference between myself and others,
So let me make others joyfully happy."

This verse expresses the attitude that lies at the heart of a Bodhisattva, one who aspires to attain enlightenment for the welfare of others. Because of a deep feeling for the essential oneness of all beings, the Bodhisattva has a profound recognition that all suffering, from the personal to the global, arises from self-concern. The Bodhisattva also knows that all happiness and well-being arises from concern and compassion for others. Such a person completely dedicates their every action and thought to bring maximum benefit and happiness to all beings without exception.

THE VENERABLE LUNGRIG NAMGYAL

*

The purpose of Islam's ethical regulations is to ensure that the natural world upon which we depend for our sustenance comes through time and changes in our technology and fashion in a flourishing condition ready to sustain the generations who come after us. Islam is the worldview that tells us that if we live wisely we must indeed live well. It is a guidance for how to walk the path of life, through change and turmoil and new possibilities, and maintain balance and harmony. Islam is about how we manage the risks of living, which are always with us, to bring forth the greatest good for humanity and nature, which is the only practical way we can demonstrate our worship for the God who made us.

*

But Islam is the challenge of living. It has furnished us with the values to face that challenge. For a believing Muslim, it becomes a matter of faith to meet the challenge of creating a just and equitable, beautiful and humane, integrated and environmentally sound society.

'And God has made the earth for you as a carpet (spread out), That ye may go about therein, in spacious roads.' (Surah LXXI: 19–20)

H.E. DR. ABDULLAH OMAR NASSEEF

Through the workings of his Spirit, Christ's tree extends its roots to the whole cosmos. In the words of St Paul, 'creation itself will be set free from its bondage to decay and will obtain the glorious liberty of the children of God' (Romans 8:21).

*

Christians therefore believe that the reconciled world, the new creation, has already been realised in and through Christ, and that it now awaits with eager longing the revelation of the glorious liberty of the children of God.

Only the sinful failure to abide in God's love and to live according to his wisdom can blind men and women to the harmonious beauty of all God's creatures. That disobedience can also lead them to sow disharmony, injustice, destruction and death, now and in the future.

FATHER SERRINI

*

From the conservationist viewpoint, the ideal situation would be one in which a profound reverence for life pervades our consciousness, manifesting itself in a deep compassion for all living creatures. Indeed the elements – the earth, the sun and the moon, the mountains and forests, the air and the water – would all be looked upon as manifestations of the divine grace.

The basic concept of Hinduism is that the divine is both immanent and transcendent; it follows that the ideal human condition would be one in which all human beings are imbued with this awareness. In that happy situation, not only would man's rapacious exploitation of Mother Earth and all its treasures give way to a creative symbiosis between man and nature, it would also put a stop to the terrible conflicts within mankind that have disfigured this earth ever since the dawn of history. Deeply aware that all creatures represent varying manifestations of the same divine power, the conflicts and turmoils which we have witnessed so far would disappear, and in their place would emerge a great spiritual commonwealth of mankind.

H.E. DR KARAN SINGH

*

The essential thrust of these teachings is that animals, even the most powerful among them, are ultimately helpless before people. We rule their kingdom, as God rules ours. The way that we exercise our power over the rest of God's creatures, over those who ultimately cannot defend themselves against us, must be the way of love and compassion. If it is not, then we ourselves have made the choice that the strong can do what they like to other living beings – and to each other. If such policies prevail, the world will soon be destroyed – by us.

*

Rabbinic courts enforced, as law, the biblical injunctions about defending the physical environment. It is forbidden, to everyone, to cut down fruit-bearing trees. It makes no difference whether the circumstances included the necessities of war, even of a supposedly righteous war, (Deuteronomy 20:19–20). The rebirth of nature, day after day, is God's gift, but humanity is the custodian of this capacity of the earth to renew itself. As we consume any one of the products of divine bounty, we must first say the appropriate grace. The world is His, and we are but sojourners. At very least, we must leave the palace of our Host no worse than we found it.

*

Our highest responsibility to our own very nature is to spend our lives, all our lives, everyone and everywhere, in helping to make order where chaos still reigns. All humanity are our brothers and sisters. All animals are in this world because God willed them, as He willed us. He is the architect and builder of the universe, of all living forms on this planet. He promised Noah after the Flood that he would never destroy this world again – but we can. Nuclear dangers are not our only problem. More insidiously, we keep turning forest into desert, by despoiling nature for our immediate advantage. We do not really think of the consequences for our children and grandchildren.

RABBI HERTZBERG

*

THE
SENDING
FORTH

WE came to Assisi to find vision and hope. Vision to discover a new and caring relationship with the rest of our living world, and hope that the destruction of nature can be stopped before all is wasted and lost.

I believe that today, in this famous shrine of the saint of ecology, a new and powerful alliance has been forged between the forces of religion and the forces of conservation. I am convinced that secular conservation has learnt to see the problems of the natural world from a different perspective and, I hope and believe, that the spiritual leaders have learnt that the natural world of Creation cannot be saved without their active involvement. Neither can ever be quite the same again.

HRH THE DUKE OF EDINBURGH

These are selections from the "Assisi Liturgy".

STORIES
MYTHS
AND
LEGENDS

BUDDHISM

A large festival was being celebrated in the kingdom of Banaras. The king's gardener wished to join the merry-makers. So he told the king of the monkeys, who lived in the garden, "Today I will go and enjoy the festivities. While I am away, please water all the plants."

The monkeys took hold of the watering pots and their king instructed them, "Do not waste any water. Pull out each plant and examine the roots. Give more water to the bigger roots and less to the smaller." The monkeys did just what their king asked them to do.

When the gardener returned, he was greatly shocked to see the dead plants. "Why have you pulled out the plants?" he cried.

"We wanted to save the water for you", replied the monkey king.

The gardener could only blame himself for having left the garden in charge of the monkeys who knew nothing of that kind of work. Though they had meant to do good, the monkeys had done a great deal of harm and had destroyed all the plants.

*

Near the Himalayan mountains there was a grove of fig trees. On one of them there lived a parrot. He spent his days eating the sweet fruit off the tree and drinking water from the Ganges. He was very content and happy.

A deva once came upon the bird and wished to test him. So using his magical powers he dried up the tree and it became a stump with large gaping holes. Dust started to blow through these holes. The parrot however continued to live on the tree, eating a bit of dust now and again, and never once complained.

The deva saw this, but wanted to test the parrot further. He changed himself into a beautiful goose and went up to the parrot. "You will starve to death if you stay on that tree any longer. Why don't you leave this stump and look for a home elsewhere on a better tree?"

"This tree has been my friend all my life. He has fed me and looked after me. How can I leave him now that he can be of no more use to me?" was the parrot's reply.

The deva was very pleased with the parrot's reply and he said, "Oh faithful bird, I am a deva. Ask me for any boon and I shall give it to you."

"Divine one! I only want my friend the fig tree to live once more and be full of strength, bearing leaves and fruit."

The deva smiled. He brought some water from the Ganges and splashed the tree with it. The rotten stump shot up and spread out its branches full of sweet fruit, leaves and flowers.

The parrot was delighted to see the tree well once more and thanked the deva again and again.

*

On the southern shore of a large lake there lived a hawk. On the western side lived a pair of hawks; on the northern, a lion; and on the eastern, an osprey. In the middle of the lake lived a tortoise.

The two hawks built their nest on a small island in the lake, on a kadamba tree. Soon two young were hatched.

One day a group of villagers went fishing in the lake, but after many hours could find nothing. They reached the island and rested under the kadamba tree. There were many mosquitoes around so they kindled a fire to drive them away.

The smoke from this fire disturbed the young hawks who were sitting in their nest, and they began to cry. The villagers heard them and said, "There are birds up on this tree. Let's catch them and roast them for our meal."

The mother bird heard them and her heart was filled with fear. "We must ask our good neighbours to help us. Only they can get us out of this trouble," she cried, and sent her husband to the osprey.

When the osprey heard of the trouble he said, "Leave it to me. I shall do all I can to help you." He rushed to the lake, soaked his wings with water, filled his beak and spilt it all over the fire. The fire immediately went out.

But the men relighted the fire. The osprey again went and brought some water to put it out. The men lighted the fire once again. This went on for some time and the osprey was getting very tired. His feathers were also burnt here and there, and he felt as if he could not fly any longer.

The hawk saw this and flew to the tortoise to ask for his help. The tortoise rushed and gathered some mud from the lake. He flung it on the fire and the fire went out.

The villagers spied the tortoise and said amongst themselves, "Let's catch this tortoise instead of the birds and roast him for our meal." They tried their best to tie the tortoise up with creepers and to roll him towards the fire. But the tortoise was too strong and dragged them towards the lake.

The men finally gave up the attempt and returned to the tree. Once again they lit a fire. The mother hawk got alarmed and cried, "Our only hope is the lion. Hurry and tell him of the danger."

The father hawk rushed up to the lion and

said, "Oh king of all beasts, please save our young ones from these evil men." The lion listened to his tale and ran to the lake. He stood there and roared.

The men became very frightened. "All the birds and animals here have been working against us and now the lion has come to kill us." They climbed into their boat and, reaching the opposite shore, ran away as fast as their legs could carry them.

The mother hawk was very happy to see the villagers leave. She flapped her wings joyously and said to her young, "My little ones, did you see how quickly our neighbours came to our help? They are true friends. We need not fear any enemy while they are with us."

*

Once the Bodhisattva, the Future Buddha, was incarnated as a deer. From the moment of his birth it was obvious that he was different: his skin had a golden radiance, his eyes were like jewels, his horns were silver, his mouth was red, his hooves were like lacquer, he had a tail like a yak's, and he was as large as a foal. On maturity he became king of a herd of five hundred deer.

In that same forest there was another golden deer called Branch, who also was the leader of a large herd. Both deer were wise and virtuous leaders. Unfortunately however the king of Banaras was very fond of venison, and every day he would send his subjects hunting for a deer from the forest. The people objected to this because they were not able to get on with their own work done, so they built a large corral in the royal park and herded the deer into it. The king was very pleased about this.

Each day the king or his butcher would go to the corral and shoot arrows into a deer until it died of exhaustion: there was no escape. The two golden deer were granted immunity however, because the king was so impressed by their magnificence. In order to save their herds from unnecessary suffering the two stags decided that each day one deer would be chosen by lot, from each herd alternately, and that deer would voluntarily put its head on the block when the king or butcher arrived.

One day the lot fell upon a pregnant doe, who went to Branch, the leader of her herd, begging that another deer be substituted, as if she were permitted to live there would be an extra deer in the herd. Branch said that he could not ask another deer to take her place, so in desperation she went to the other golden stag, the Bodhisattva, who assured her that another deer would take her place.

When the butcher came the Bodhisattva put his own head on the block. The king was called, and he asked the stag why he was volunteering his life when he had been given immunity. The stag explained about the pregnant doe and said that he could not ask

another deer to take her place so he himself was ready to die to save her.

The king said that even amongst humans he had never seen such love and compassion, and spared the lives of both the stag and the doe. The stag asked about the other deer in the park, and the king agreed to spare them as well. The stag then asked about the other deer in the forest, and the king also granted them immunity. The golden stag continued until he had received from the king a promise of immunity for all the creatures of the forests, birds of the air, and fish of the waters.

Having converted the king from the violent ways of a hunter to the way of compassion and non-injury to any form of life, which is the first of the five great rules of mortality, the golden stag continued to preach to the king about the other virtues. The golden stag remained in the park for a few days teaching righteousness to the king with the ease and skill of a Buddha, and then he departed for the forest to live in peace with his herd. Meanwhile the king followed the wise teaching of the Bodhisattva and was suitably rewarded after death.

CHRISTIANITY

Long ago there was a violent, aggressive and destructive knight by the name of Sir Hubert. He took pleasure in causing pain and distress to all God's creatures, both human and animal. He loved to hunt and was merciless in his pursuit of prey. He was proud and bombastic by nature, and terrorised the villages around his castle by his capricious behaviour. His servants and squires lived in dread of his temper, and few there were who counted themselves as his friend. Nor had he any respect for Christ or His Church. He rarely attended church and paid no heed to the attempts of the local clergy to calm his wildness or abuses of power.

One day he rose and decided to go hunting. His servants were aghast, for this was no ordinary day. This was Good Friday, the very day upon which Our Lord had been crucified and died for our sins. Surely today of all days Sir Hubert would not seek to kill any of God's creatures? But no: he was determined to have his way, and the hunt made ready.

Through the castle gates streamed the pack with the hunters close behind. Soon they left the path and galloped across the meadows towards the forest. Then on the edge of the forest they caught sight of a magnificent stag who, hearing the baying of the hounds, turned and vanished into the denseness of the forest.

But the hounds picked up his scent and were off. Behind them rode Hubert, with a fury such as few had seen before. Soon he had left his servants and squires far behind as he and his horse crashed on through the forest.

Hubert knew the forest well and saw that the hounds were driving the stag into a corner of the forest where sheer cliffs made escape impossible. With grim determination Hubert spurred on his horse. Sure enough, he saw the hounds turn towards the cliff face and he knew that through the next line of trees he would see the stag at bay. But what he actually saw shook him. For there against the cliff face was the stag. But instead of the hounds snapping and snarling at the beast, they lay motionless and soundless on the grass. Then, to Hubert's astonishment, his horse knelt to the ground, throwing the knight on to the turf. It was only when Hubert stood up and looked properly at the stag that he began to understand. For there, set between the great creature's antlers, was a crucifix. Hubert fell to his knees hardly daring to look upon this, the Golgatha of his own making; the Passiontide of his own anger; the evidence of his cruelty and sin.

They found him, hours later, still kneeling and praying. He wept as they carried him home, and for days he would not venture from his room. Then one day, like Christ from His tomb, Hubert came out. But this was not the old Hubert: for now he wore the simple gown of a lowly priest. He gave away all that he had to the poor and became in later years a great missionary. In churches dedicated to him his symbol may be seen: the symbol of how creation spoke for its creator – the symbol of the stag with the crucifix.

*

In the forests outside the town of Arles (in southern France) there dwelt a hermit by the name of Giles. He lived his life simply in prayer and meditation and was trusted by the creatures of the forest, for he never harmed them.

Amongst the animals there was one especially close to Giles: a young hind. One day Wamba, king of the Visigoths, came riding into the forest to hunt. The hounds found the scent of the young hind and the chase was on. The terrified deer turned and ran towards where she knew Giles would be. But the hounds began to gain on her and the king himself led the hunters crashing through the undergrowth. With one last desperate leap the hind broke through the bushes into the clearing where Giles was in prayer, but not before the king had loosed an arrow which sped through the air after the disappearing deer.

When the king rode into the clearing his hounds fell back, unable to move forward, as though restrained by some greater power. And there, standing with his arms holding the hind, stood Giles, the arrow having pierced his protecting hands but having failed to touch the hind. The king fell to the ground begging for forgiveness, and from that day on he eschewed hunting and followed the way of Christ.

*

During the period when St Francis was living in Gubbio there appeared a very fierce and terrible wolf, which devoured not only animals but also men and women. Everyone leaving the city went armed, and no man travelling alone was safe from the wolf. Eventually people became so frightened that they did not dare to leave the city.

St Francis, having compassion on them, determined against their advice to meet the wolf. Putting his trust in God he left the city with his companions. When the companions had gone as far as they dared St Francis went on alone to the wolf's territory. As the wolf ran towards him, St Francis went to meet him making the sign of the cross, and commanding him in Christ's name not to harm him or any other person. In that instant the wolf stopped

running, and came like a lamb and laid himself down at the feet of St Francis.

St Francis told the wolf that he had committed great crimes in killing God's creatures without His permission; but worse than that, he had also dared to kill men, made in the image of God, and had therefore earned the hatred and enmity of everyone in the city. St Francis asked him to make peace with the people of the city, so that they would forgive him. By bowing his head the wolf showed that he accepted this, and St Francis promised that if the wolf kept peace with the people he would see that they fed him for as long as he lived, so that he would no longer suffer hunger; for he realised that the wolf had killed only through hunger. In return he required the wolf's promise that he would never again harm any human being or animal, and again the wolf indicated his acceptance by bowing his head. The wolf lifted his fore-foot and put it into the hand of St Francis as a binding token of obedience and trust.

Then St Francis led the wolf, now gentle as a lamb, back to the city, to the great amazement of all the people. He told them what he had promised the wolf, in return for the wolf's promise not to harm any person or any animal, and said that he stood surety for the wolf's observance of this covenant. Then everyone promised that they would provide food for the wolf, and by placing his fore-foot into the hand of St Francis the wolf again showed to all the people his willingness to abide by this agreement. At this the people were filled with joy and admiration for St Francis, for the miracle and for the peace with the wolf, and they rejoiced greatly and praised God.

The wolf lived peacefully in Gubbio for two years, going from door to door in friendliness, and the inhabitants fed him courteously. He harmed no one, nor any animal, and the dogs did not bark after him. When he died the citizens were very sorry, because as the wolf went gently about their city he had reminded them of the virtue and sanctity of St Francis.[90]

HINDUISM

Narada Muni saw that a deer was lying on the path through the forest and that it was pierced by an arrow. It had broken legs and was twisting much due to pain. Farther ahead, Narada Muni saw a boar pierced by an arrow. Its legs were also broken, and it was twisting in pain. When he went farther, he saw a rabbit that was also suffering. Narada Muni was greatly pained at heart to see living entities suffer so. When Narada Muni advanced farther, he saw a hunter behind a tree. This hunter was holding arrows, and he was ready to kill more animals. The hunter's body was blackish. He had reddish eyes, and he appeared fierce. It was as if the superintendent of death, Yamaraja was standing there with bows and arrows in his hands. When Narada Muni left the forest path and went to the hunter all the animals immediately saw him and fled. When all the animals fled, the hunter wanted to chastise Narada with abusive language, but due to Narada's presence, he could not utter anything abusive.

The hunter addressed Narada Muni: 'O gosvani! O great saintly person! Why have you left the general path through the forest to come to me? Simply by seeing you, all the animals I was hunting have now fled'.

Narada Muni replied, 'Leaving the path, I have come to you to settle a doubt that is in my mind. I was wondering whether all the boars and other animals that are half killed belong to you.'

The Hunter replied, 'Yes, what you are saying is so'.

Narada Muni then inquired, 'Why did you not kill the animals completely? Why did you half-kill them by piercing their bodies with arrows?'

The Hunter replied, "My dear saintly person, my name is Marigari, enmity of animals. My father taught me to kill them in that way. When I see half killed animals suffer, I get great pleasure'.

Narada Muni then told the Hunter, 'I have one thing to beg of you'.

The Hunter replied, 'You may take whatever animals or anything else you would like. I have many skins. If you would like them I shall give you either a deer skin or a tiger skin'.

Narada Muni said, 'I do not want any of the skins. I am only asking one thing from you in charity. I beg you that from this day on, you will kill animals completely and not leave them half dead.'

The Hunter replied, 'My dear sir, what are you asking of me? What is wrong with animals lying half killed? Will you please explain this to me?'

Narada Muni replied, 'If you leave the animals half dead you are purposefully giving them pain. Therefore you will have to suffer in retaliation. My dear Hunter, your business is killing animals. That is a slight offence on your part, but when you consciously give them unnecessary pain by leaving them half dead you incur very great sin. All the animals you have killed and given unnecessary pain will kill you one after the other in your next life and in life after life'.

In this way through the association of the great sage Narada Muni, the Hunter was convinced of his sinful activity. He therefore became somewhat afraid due to his offences.

The Hunter then admitted that he was convinced of his sinful activity and he said, 'I have been taught this business from my very childhood. Now I am wondering how I can become free from these unlimited volumes of sinful activity. My dear Sir, please tell me how I can be relieved from the reactions of my sinful life. How can I fully surrender on to you and fall down at your lotus feet. Please deliver me from sinful reactions'.

Narada Muni assured the Hunter, 'If you listen to my instructions, I shall find the way that you can be liberated.'

The Hunter then said, 'My dear sir, whatever you say I shall do.'

Narada Muni immediately ordered him, 'First of all break your bow, then I shall tell you what is to be done'.

The hunter replied, 'If I break my bow, how shall I maintain myself?'

Narada Muni replied, 'Do not worry, I shall supply all your food everyday.'

Being reassured by the great sage Narada Muni, the Hunter broke his bow and immediately fell down at Saint's lotus feet and fully surrendered. After this, Narada Muni raised him with his hand and gave him instructions for spiritual advancement.

Narada Muni then advised the Hunter, 'Return home and distribute whatever riches you have to the pure Brahmins who know the absolute truth. After distributing all your riches to the Brahmins, both you and your wife should leave home, taking only one cloth to wear'.

Narada Muni continued, 'Leave your home and go to the river. There you should construct a small cottage and in front of the cottage you should grow a "tulsi" plant on a raised platform. After planting the "tulsi" tree before your house, you shall daily circumambulate that "tulsi" plant. Serve her by giving her water and other things and continually chant the 'Hare Krishna Mahamantra". Narada Muni continued, 'I shall send sufficient food to you both everyday. You can take as much food as you want'.

The three animals that were half killed were then brought to consciousness by the sage Narada. Indeed, the animals got up and swiftly fled.

When the Hunter saw the half killed animals flee, he was certainly struck with wonder. He then offered his respectful obeisance to the sage Narada and returned home. After all this Narada Muni went to his destination. After the Hunter returned hom, he followed exactly the instructions of his spiritual master, Narada. The news that the Hunter had become a Vaishnav spread all over the village. Indeed, all the villagers brought arms and presented them to the Vaishnav who was formally a hunter. In one day enough food was brought for ten to twenty people, but the Hunter and his wife would accept only as much as they could eat.

One day, while speaking to his friend, Parvata Muni, Narada Muni requested to go with him to see his disciple, the Hunter. When the Saintly sages came to Hunter's place, the Hunter could see them coming from a distance with great clarity. The Hunter began to run towards his spiritual master, but he could not fall down and offer his obeisance because ants were running hither and tither around his feet. Seeing the ants, the Hunter whisked them away with a piece of cloth. After clearing the ants from the ground, he fell down flat to offer his obeisance. Narada Muni said, 'My dear Hunter, such behaviour is not at all astonishing. A man in devotional service is automatically non-violent. He is the best of gentleman.[91]

*

Long ago, when Brahmadatta was king of Benares, there came this thought into his mind: "Everywhere in India there are kings whose palaces have many columns; what if I build a palace supported by a single column only? Then shall I be the first and singular king among all other kings." So he summoned his craftsmen, and ordered them to build him a magnificent palace supported by a single pillar. "It shall be done." they said: and away they went into the forest.

There they found a tree, tall and straight, worthy to be the single pillar of such a palace. But the road was too rough and the distance too great for them to take the trunk to the city, so they returned to the king and asked him what was to be done. "Somehow or other," he said, "you must bring it, and that without delay." But they answered that neither somehow nor anyhow could it be done. "Then," said the king, "you must select a tree in my own park."

There they found a lordly sal-tree, straight and beautiful, worshipped alike by village and town and royal family. They told the king, and he said to them: "Good, go and fell the tree at once." But they could not do this without making the customary offerings to the tree-god living there, and asking him to depart. So they made offerings of flowers and branches and lighted lamps, and said to the tree: "On the seventh day from this we shall fell the tree, by the king's command. Let any deva that may be dwelling in the tree depart elsewhere, and not unto us be the blame!" The god that dwelt in the tree heard what they said, and considered thus: "These craftsmen are agreed to fell my tree. I myself shall perish when my home is destroyed. All the young sal-trees round me will be destroyed as well, in which many devas of my kith and kin are living. My own death touches me not so nearly as the destruction of my children, so let me, if possible, save their lives at least."

So at the hour of midnight the tree-god, divinely radiant, entered the king's resplendent chamber, his glory lighting up the whole room.

The king was startled, and stammered out: "What being art thou, so god-like and so full of grief?" The deva-prince replied: "I am called in thy realm, O king, the Lucky-tree; for sixty thousand years all men have loved and worshipped me. Many a house and many a town, many a palace too, they made, yet never did me wrong; honour thou me, even as did they, O king!" But the king answered that such a tree was just what he needed for his palace, a trunk so fine and tall and straight; and in that palace, said he, "thou shalt long endure, admired of all who behold thee." The tree-god answered: "If it must be so, then I have one boon to ask: cut first the top, the middle next, and then the root of me." The king protested that this was a more painful death than to be felled entire. "O forest lord," he said, "what gain is thine thus to be cut limb from limb and piece by piece?" To which the Lucky-tree replied: "There is a good reason for my wish: my kith and kin have grown up round me, beneath my shade, and I should crush them if I fall entire upon them, and they would grieve exceedingly."

At this the king was deeply moved, and wondered at the tree-god's noble thought, and lifting his hands in salutation, he said: "O Lucky-tree, O forest lord, as thou wouldst save thy kindred, so shall I spare thee; so fear nothing."

Then the tree-god gave the king good counsel and went his way; and the king next day gave generous alms, and ruled as became a king until the time came for his departure to the heavenly world. [92]

*

The Prophet and his companions once paused during a journey, and made a camp where they could rest. The Prophet went round the camp, talking to the men, and making sure that everything was all right.

Then, not far away, he saw a fire. Someone had lit the fire to keep himself warm. The Prophet walked over towards the man who had lit the fire, to talk with him.

Suddenly, he saw that not far away, there was an ant hill. The ants could be seen running about near the hill, working very hard, as ants do. Some of the ants were further away from the ant hill than others, and the Prophet saw that they were getting very close to the fire the man had lit. If they came much closer, the ants might be burned up or harmed in some way.

The Prophet was very disturbed to see this. The ants were in danger. That meant that God's living creatures were in danger. "Who has made fire here?" he asked.

The man who had made the fire looked up. "I made the fire, O, Messenger of Allah!" he replied. "It is cold and I needed to make myself warm."

"Quick!" the Prophet told him. "Put out the fire!" "Put out the fire!"

The man obeyed at once. He took a blanket and beat the fire until its flames died away.

Then, the man looked round and saw that there were ants near to where the fire had been. He realised then that the Prophet had been worried about the ants. He did not want the fire to hurt them and in his great mercy had ordered the fire to be put out.

Ever afterwards, the man always remembered to look round carefully before he made a fire.

"There might be ants or other animals nearby," he said to himself. "And Allah forbids that any man should hurt them!"[93]

One day Muhammad was travelling with some friends. When they stopped for a rest, Muhammad went off by himself for a while. His friends saw a mother bird and her young ones flying in the sky. The friends decided to catch the young birds to amuse themselves. It didn't take very long because the young birds were not very good at flying. Soon the birds were caught, and the men enjoyed feeling the birds struggling against their hands. But when Muhammad returned he was angry. He could see that the mother bird was upset. He ordered his friends to let the young birds go. Their selfish pleasure had caused great unhappiness to the birds, and that was wrong. [94]

*

There was a little boy in Madina who was a good boy, except for one very bad habit. He used to throw stones at trees, and what is more, he enjoyed doing it.

One day the boy went into an oasis that lay outside Madina. He found date trees growing in the cool, shady oasis and as soon as he saw them he picked up some stones and started throwing them. The stones hit the palm trees and the dates fell down into the sand. After a while, the boy stopped throwing stones, and started doing something else he enjoyed very much: that was eating the dates which he had knocked down from the trees.

The dates tasted delicious and the boy ate them all, giving no thought at all to the damage he might have caused the trees. He did not think either about the owners of the trees. They became very angry when they found out what the boy had done. The owners of the trees knew that the boy would come back to the oasis to throw more stones and eat more dates as they fell to the ground. So they lay in wait for him.

Sure enough, the boy arrived, threw stones at the trees and then gathered up the dates that had fallen down. The owners of the trees rushed out and, before the boy could get away, they grabbed him. The boy was very frightened and

alarmed, but however hard he struggled and however loudly he yelled he could not escape the grasp of the men who had caught him.

The men took the boy to the Prophet and told him what the boy had done. The boy stood before the Prophet feeling very frightened. He was certain the Prophet would be angry with him. But the Prophet spoke to him in a quiet, soft voice that had no anger in it.

'Why do you throw stones at the trees?' the Prophet wanted to know.

'To get the dates to eat.' the boy replied. 'If I don't make dates fall from the trees, how am I going to get them?'

This reply showed that the boy was only a child who did not understand a great deal, and had a lot to learn in life. The Prophet realised this at once. He realised, too, that the boy had not been wicked, but just foolish and a little stupid.

So the Prophet patted the boy on the head to calm his fears and spoke kindly to him. 'Don't throw stones at the trees,' he said to the boy. 'For if the trees are damaged, they will not bring forth new fruit. Eat of the dates that have already fallen to the ground.'

Then the Prophet blessed the boy and prayed that he would soon gain wisdom and be more sensible in the future. [95]

*

Once when the Master, the holy Ari, was sitting in the House of Study with his disciples he looked at one of them and said to him: 'Go out from here, for today you are excommunicated from heaven.' The disciple fell at the feet of the Master and said to him: 'What is my sin? I will repent for it.'

So the Master said to him: "It is because of the chickens you have at home. You have not fed them for two days and they cry out to God in their hunger. God will forgive you on condition you see to it that before you leave for prayers in the morning you give food to your chickens. For they are dumb animals and they cannot ask for their food." [96]

*

The Sassover was accustomed to attend county fairs, and there to do good offices to those in need. Once it befell that some cattle breeders had left their animals standing in the market-place with their thirst unslaked, while their owners attended to their affairs elsewhere. The Sassover, perceiving this, made the rounds with a bucket and gave the calves their drink. A dealer, returning from an errand and seeing a stranger thus employed, mistook him for a hired man, and commanded him to give drink to his cattle. The Rabbi obeyed, and, after having performed his chore, was offered a coin. He laughingly refused, saying: "Get thee hence, man; I did not do thy bidding, but God's, Who commands us to be merciful to His creatures."[97]

*

I heard from the Rabbi of the Holy Community of Polonnoye and from the rabbi of our community that Rabbi Nahman of Kosov had a relative named Rabbi Yudel of Chudnov, whose father, Rabbi Joseph, was a preacher.

It was Rabbi Yudel's way not to accept favours from other people. He enjoyed the fruit of his own labour. He was in the iron ore business.

Once he went to a mine where he wanted to keep the Sabbath. The householder said to him: "What will you eat, sir? I do not have fish, and you would not eat the meat because you did not examine the knife. I advise you to go to another mine nearby where there is a wealthy man, and he certainly will have fish and a shohet. You, sir, can go to this man." And so he did.

Near the mine the road passed through a pond. The water was not usually deep, but when it rained or when the snow melted the pond became deeper. Rabbi Yudel was not aware of this and he wanted to go across. A dog ran forward into the pond and sank in the water. The dog was drowning and it howled pitifully. Its cries stirred the heart of the Hasid and tears fell from his eyes. He saw that it was impossible to go across the water, and he returned to the mine and asked the householder to do everything possible to bring fish for the Sabbath. The householder went to urge the fishermen and they caught a large pike.

The householder said: "I have lived in this village for several years and I have never seen such a fish." They prepared several dishes from it.

On the Sabbath eve Rabbi Yudel was sitting by the table singing songs, and he fell asleep with his head on the table. His father appeared to him in his dream and said: "Know that I was reincarnated as that fish. The informer who I always condemned during my life was reincarnated as the dog that drowned. His redemption was that he drowned in order to save you. I was reincarnated as this fish because I persecuted him. The tears that you shed when the dog drowned redeemed me. Be careful, my son, how you eat this fish."

When he came to the Besht, the Besht told him that he used to say that Rabbi Yudel was a reincarnation of Samuel the Prophet.[98]

*

Rab Huna and Rab Hisda were seated together. Gneiba passed by, and the one Rabbi said to the other: "Let us rise before him because he is a sage."

The other answered: "Shall we rise up before a quarrelsome person, who torments Mar Ukbah, the Chief Justice?"

Gneiba halted, however, and took his seat near them, and said: "Greetings to you, O Kings!"

The Rabbis asked: "Why do you greet us so?"

Gneiba replied: "Because we read in Proverbs 8:15: 'By me (learning or wisdom) kings reign.'"

They invited him into the house and set food before him. He said: "I have not yet fed my beast, and Rab Judah has said in the name of Rab that a man is forbidden to eat unless he has fed his beasts, as it is written (Deut. 11:15): 'I will give grass in thy fields for thy cattle, and thou shalt eat and be satisfied.'"[99]

*

"The Lord is good to all; and His tender mercies are over all His works." (Ps. 145:9)

The Patriarch, Rabbi Judah I, suffered from toothache for many years. Why was he thus punished? Because he once saw a bound calf being taken to the slaughter. The calf bleated and appealed for his aid, but the Rabbi said: "Go, since it is for this that thou hast been created."

And how was the Patriarch cured? He once saw a litter of mice being carried to the river to be drowned. He said: "Let them go free, for it is written that 'His mercies are over all His works.'"[100]

CHINESE

Mr Kuo of the Ch'i state was very rich, while Mr Hsiang of the Sung state was very poor. Mr Hsiang travelled from Sung to Ch'i and asked the other for the secret of his prosperity. Mr Kuo told him, "It is because I am a good thief. The first year I began to be a thief, I had just enough. The second year, I had ample. The third year, I reaped a great harvest. And, in the course of time, I found myself the owner of whole villages and districts."

Mr Hsiang was overjoyed; he understood the word "thief" in its literal sense, but he did not understand the true way of becoming a thief. Accordingly, he climbed over walls and broke into houses, grabbing everything he could see or lay hands upon. But before very long his thefts brought him into trouble, and he was stripped of even what he had previously possessed. Thinking that Mr Kuo had basely deceived him, Hsiang went to him with a bitter complaint.

"Tell me," said Mr Kuo, "how did you set about being a thief?" On learning from Mr Hsiang what had happened, he cried out: "Alas and alack! You have been brought to this pass because you went the wrong way to work. Now let me put you on the right track. We all know that Heaven has its seasons, and that earth has its riches. Well, the things that I steal are the riches of Heaven and earth, each in their season – the fertilizing rain water from the clouds, and the natural products of mountain and meadow land. Thus I grow my grain and ripen my crops, build my walls and construct my tenements. From the dry land I steal winged and four-footed game, from the rivers I steal fish and turtles. There is nothing that I do not steal. For corn and grain, clay and wood, birds and beasts, fishes and turtles are all products of nature. How can I claim them as mine?

"Yet, stealing in this way from Providence, I bring on myself no retribution. Gold, jade, and precious stones, corn, silk stuffs, and all manner of riches are simply appropriated by men. How can Providence be said to give them away? Yet if we commit a crime in stealing them, who is there to resent it?"

Mr Hsiang, in a state of great perplexity, and fearing to be led astray a second time by Mr Kuo, went off to consult Tung Kuo, a man of learning. Tung Kuo said to him: "Are you not already a thief in respect of your own body? You are stealing the harmony of the Yin and the Yang in order to keep alive and maintain your bodily form. How much more, then, are you a thief with regard to external possessions! Assuredly, Heaven and earth cannot be dissociated from the myriad objects of nature. To claim any one of these as your own betokens confusion of thought. Mr Kuo's thefts are carried out in a spirit of self-seeking, and therefore landed you in trouble. Those who take possession of property, whether public or private, are thieves. Those who abstain from taking property, public or private, are also thieves. The great principle of Heaven and earth is to treat public property as such and private property as such. Knowing this principle, which of us is a thief, and at the same time which of us is not a thief?"[101]

*

On the occasion of the first day of the year the people of Hantan offered a wild duck to Prince Chien of Chao. The Prince was well pleased and rewarded the men amply. One of his guests asked to know the reason why. Prince Chien said, "To set free a live bird on New Year's Day is to do an extraordinarily good deed." The guest said, "If the people know that their prince loves to set birds free they will vie with one another in catching them from him, and many birds will therefore be killed. If you really wish to see the birds live you would do better forbidding the people to catch them. When you catch a bird in order to set it free again, your good deed and bad cancel each other."[102]

*

Chuang tzu was about to die, and his disciples wanted to give him a sumptuous funeral. Chuang tzu said: 'I would like heaven and earth for my inner and outer coffins; the sun and the moon to be my jade disks; the host of stars to be my pearly ornaments; and all creation to be my 'sending off' gifts. Are not the furnishings of my funeral already prepared? How can anything be added to these?' The disciples answered: 'We fear that the kites will feed on our Master.' Then Chuang tzu said: 'Above ground I should be eaten by kites, below ground by ants. Would it not be unfair to take from the one in order to give to the other?'[103]

LET ME HARKEN TO THAT BIRD
THAT BELL VOICED TUI-BIRD
WHO CRIES UNITE UNITE
LET UNITY PREVAIL
UNITE THE HEAVENLY REALM
WITH THE EARTHLY REALM
UNITE THE OUTERMOST
EXTENTS OF THE UNIVERSE
WITH THE INNERMOST
RECESSES OF MEN'S HEARTS
ONLY THE NIGHT CAN SEE
THE UNITY OF MAN
WITH ALL THAT SURROUNDS
GLORY HALLELUJAH

REFERENCES
TO THE
TEXTS

SELECTIONS FROM THE
SCRIPTURES

1   Quoted in "Sayings of the Buddha",
    Sheldon Press, London

2   Ditto

3   The Tathagata as a rain-cloud:
    Saddharmapundarika V v.26, 36–38.
    From "Buddhist Texts through the
    Ages", ed. E. Conze, Harper
    Torchbooks 1964

4   Vinaya Pitaka Mahavagga iii. I

5   Sikshasamuccaya 280–81
    (Vajradhvaja Sutra)

6   Culla-Vagga v 6

7   Theragatha. Tran. K.R. Norman,
    pp.97–98, The Pali Text Society,
    London 1969

8   Anguttara Nikaya, Gradual Sayings,
    Vol.3 p.262

9   Digha-Nikaya Vol. III pp.81–82. Trans.
    T.W. Rhys Davids, The Pali Text
    Society, London 1965

10 Gospel of Matthew 6 vv.25–33

11 Gospel of John 1 vv.1–5

12 Paul's Letter to the Romans, 8 vv.18–25

13 Book of Revelation 21 vv.1–7

14 Book of Revelation 11 v.18

15 Creation Hymn – Rig Ved.a x vv.1–7.
    Trans. Dr. Yamini Krishnamurti

16 Katha Upanishad IV vv.7–11. Trans.
    Juan Mascaro, "The Upanishads",
    Penguin Classics. 1965

17 Katha Upanishad, op.cit.

18 Svetasvatara Upanishad, op.cit.

19 Chandogya Upanishad 8, op.cit.

20 Bhagavad-Gita VII vv.9–10 and XII
    vv.13–14. Central Chinmayer Mission
    Trust, Bombay

21 The Atharva Veda – The Vedic
    Experience: Mantramanjari: An
    Anthology of the Vedas for Modern Man
    and Contemporary Celebration. Ed. &
    trans. Raimundo Panikkar, Darton,
    Longman and Todd, 1977.
    Vv 2–5: 15–17: 35–36: 55–56: 62–63

22 The Qur'an, Surah II: 30–33

23 The Qur'an, Surah III: 190–91

24 The Qur'an, Surah VI: 38

25 The Qur'an, Surah XVI: 3–17

26 The Qur'an, Surah XX: 5–8

27 The Qur'an, Surah XXV: 47–50

28 The Qur'an, Surah XXXVIII: 27–28

29 The Qur'an, Surah LXXI: 15–20

30 The Qur'an, Surah LXXX: 24–32

31 Genesis 2: 15

32 Genesis 2: 19

33 Genesis 9: 1–17

34   Deuteronomy 20: 19

35   Job 38: 4–41

36   Psalm 8: 3–9

37   Psalm 104: 1–32

38   Psalm 148: 1–12

39   Isaiah 11: 6–9

40   Hosea 4: 1–3

41   Selections from the writings of 'Abdu'l-Bahá

42   Tablets of Bahá'u'lláh p.142

43   'Abdu'l-Bahá, Some Answered Questions, Chap. 1. p.3

44   'Abdu'l-Bahá, Some Answered Questions, Chap. XLVI p.207

45   Selections from the writings of 'Abdu'l-Bahá

46   Selections from the writings of 'Abdu'l-Bahá pp.41–42

47   Ragu Mājhu Mah. v.XXXII

48   Japji 4: 1: 18   4: 1: 21 Selection of hymns of Guru Nanak from Adi Granth. Trans. D.A.T. Thomas, Open University 1978

PRAYER AND PROSE

49   The Jātaka Vol.II, p.246. Ed. Prof. E.B. Cowell, The Pali Text Society, London 1957

50   Shantideva

51   Shutaku The Penguin Book of Zen Poetry. Ed. & trans. Lucien Stryk and Takashi Ikemoto, Allen Lane 1977 (taken from Zen: Poems, Prayers, Sermons, Anecdotes, Interviews. Trans. Stryk, Ikemoto, Doubleday, 1963, 1965)

52   Gudo (1579–1661) op.cit.

53   His Holiness the XIVth Dalai Lama: A Human Approach to World Peace p.7, Wisdom Publications, London 1984

54   Canticle of the Creatures. St Francis of Assisi, trans. Molly Reidy

55   On Prayer, XXIV, 4

56   Haxaemeron, Homily VIII, 7

57   Hexaemeron, Homily VIIII, 5

58   Hexaemeron, Homily IX, 5

59   Hexaemeron, Homily VIII, 8

60   The Great Catechism, Chapter VI

61   On the Making of Man, 11, 2

62   The Second Oration on Easter, VII

63   City of God, Book X 11, 4 and 5

64   Confessions, Book X, 6

65   St Bonaventure, "The Soul's journey into God". P.65 of classics series, SPCK. Trans. Ewert Cousins, Classics of Western Spirituality 1978

66   Jacob Boehme, "The Way to Christ", pp.92–93 in SPCK classics series, trans. Peter C. Erb, 1978

67   The Little Flowers of St Francis, pp.63–64. Trans. W. Heywood, Edizioni Porziuncola 1982

68   Srimād-Bhāgavatām Canto 7 14: 9

69   Sri Isopanishad, Mantra 1

70   A Flight of Swans. Poems from Balaka Rabindranath Tagore. Trans. Aurobindo Bose John Murray, London, 1962

71   Mahādēviyakka, Speaking of Siva. Trans. A.K. Ramaniyan, Penguin Classics 1973

72   A Source Book of Modern Hinduism. Ed. Glyn Richards, Curzen Press Ltd. 1985 (From the selected works of Mahatma Ghandhi, Ahmedabad: Navajivan Publishing House, 1969, Vol.VI)

73   Mishkat al Masabih Vol.2 p.613

74   Op.cit. Vol.1 p.600

75   Op.cit. Vol.1 p.64

76   Bukhari and Muslim – Mishkat 6: 6–7 A Manual of Hadith, Maulana Muhammad Ali, Curzon press, London and Dublin 1944, 1983 edition

77   Mahmud Shabistari, "Gulshan-i-raz", trans. E.H. Whinfield, London 1880

78 Invocation, The Conference of the Birds, Farid au⁄Din Attar. Trans. C.S. Notts, Arkana Paperbacks 1985

79 The Talmud: Teachings of the Rabbis

80 Samual Ha⁄Nagid, 993–1056 AD. The Jewish Poets of Spain. Trans. David Goldstein, Penguin Classics, London 1965

81 Joseph Ibn Abithur, c.950–1012 AD. The Jewish poets of Spain. Trans. David Goldstein

82 Taken from The Wisdom of the Jewish Mystics by Alan Unterman: Sheldon Press

83 Midrash Vayosha: Hebraic Literature. Trans. & ed. Maurice H. Harry, Tudor Publishing Co., New York, 1946

84 Midrash

85 Midrash

86 Tao Te Ching Chapter 34

87 Mencius Book VI Part 1 Chapter VIII vv.1–2

88 Chapter 9, Chuang Tzu

89 Chapter 22, Chuang Tzu: Trans. Herbert A. Giles, Mandala Books, Unwin Paperbacks, London 1961

STORIES, MYTHS AND LEGENDS

90 Little Flowers of St Francis

91 Sri Caitanya – caritāmrta – Madhya – lila Chapter 24

92 Myths of the Hindus and the Buddhists

93 Love all Creatures: M.S. Kayani, Muslim Children's Library, The Islamic Foundation 1981

94 From the Hadith, retold in Worlds of Difference, Palmer and Bisset, Blackie 1985

95 A Great Friend of Children: M.S. Kayani Muslim Children's Library, The Islamic Foundation 1981.

96 The wisdom of the Jewish Mystics. Alan Unterman, Sheldon Press 1976

97 The Hasidic Anthology, selected by Louis I. Newman Blech Publishing Company, New York, 1944

98 In Praise of the Baal Shem Tov

99 Gittin 62

100 Y. Kilaim, Chapter 9

101 Leih Tze – From Chinese Wit and Humour. Ed. George Kao. Sterling Publishing Co. Inc. (New York) 1974, pp.26–27

102 Chinese Wit and Humour. Ed. George Kao. Sterling Publishing Co. Inc. (New York) 1974 (Distributed in UK by Ward Lock)

103 From Chuang Tzu

ACKNOWLEDGEMENTS

There are so many people from all around the world who have helped with this book and with the events from which this book arose. We cannot mention them all, but there are a few who deserve special mention.

First of all we must thank our fellow workers in the World Wildlife Fund UK and in the International Consultancy on Religion, Education and Culture (ICOREC). Chief amongst these are Cherry Duggan, Pallavi Mavani, Joanne O'Brien, Liz Breuilly and Kerry Brown.

Our thanks also to the members of the different faiths who gave us so much time when we came to choosing the texts. Their patience and willingness to delve deep within their own traditions moved us all and made possible this initial taste of what the religious writings of the world have to offer us. In particular the five religious representatives at Assisi, the Venerable Lungrig Namgyal; Father Lanfranco Serrini; Dr Karan Singh; His Excellency Dr Abdullah Omar Nasseef and Rabbi Arthur Hertzberg. Others who must be mentioned are Ranchor Das, Dr Mughram, Father Bernard Przewozny OFM, Jim Belither, Dalgit Singh, Kwok Man-Ho and Hugh Locke. For the innumerable cups of tea and hours of patient explaining, thank you.

To the many authors, translators and publishers who allowed us to use their materials either free of copyright or at very reduced rates – our heartfelt gratitude.

The support and encouragement from Oliver Caldecott at Rider, Century Hutchinson made it possible to turn an idea into a reality. We hope the sales figures justify Oliver's confidence in us!

Walking with the pilgrims to Assisi were four young art students from London art colleges – Miles Aldridge, Mike Nicholson, Rachel Ross and Chris White. Their work, undertaken while walking some twenty miles each day, is used to illustrate this book.

To our friends at Omnific, especially Andrew Gossett, our gratitude for undertaking the design of this book. It is a joy to work with someone who can put across in design and image what you cannot adequately express in words.

Finally our thanks go to Kogan Page Ltd for turning the book round so fast at the last moment.

MARTIN PALMER, ANNE NASH
AND IVAN HATTINGH.

Feast Day of St Jerome, 20th July 1987.

ABOUT THE WORLD WILDLIFE FUND

CONTACTS AND FURTHER INFORMATION

The World Wildlife Fund is an international conservation foundation with national affiliates and associate organisations around the world. It was launched in 1961 to raise money for the conservation of nature, the natural environment and ecological processes essential to life on earth.

WWF aims to create awareness of threats to the natural environment, to generate and attract on a world-wide basis the strongest possible moral and financial support for safeguarding the living world and to convert such support into action based on scientific priorities.

Since its foundation WWF has spent over £81 million on around 5,000 projects in about 130 countries. About 1,500 of these are projects in the UK – WWF spends up to £650,000 on conservation and education work here each year – and now funds up to 200 different projects annually.

The money raised by WWF has protected rain forests, marshes, islands, meadow-land and coastal areas, supported scientific research into endangered species and their ecology, and funded national parks, integrated land use/resource management plans and conservation education projects all over the world. WWF has also served as a catalyst for conservation action, and brought its influence to bear on critical conservation needs by working with and influencing governments, non-governmental organisations, scientists, industry and the general public.

The network on conservation and religion publishes a quarterly magazine called "The New Road". Copies are available free from the network. Please contact

Network on Conservation and Religion,
WWF International,
World Conservation Centre,
CH-1196 Gland,
Switzerland.

The World Wildlife Fund in the UK has a continuing programme of work with religious organisations and with schools in the UK. Please contact

Ivan Hattingh,
WWF UK,
Panda House,
11–13 Ockford Road,
Godalming,
Surrey GU7 1QU,
United Kingdom.

The religious advisers to both WWF International and WWF UK are members of the International Consultancy on Religion, Education and Culture (ICOREC). For information about the conservation and religion network and associated projects with other conservation bodies and organisations please contact

Martin Palmer,
ICOREC,
Didsbury College,
Wilmslow Road,
Manchester M20 8RR,
United Kingdom.

For copies of the "Worlds of Difference" book, "Assisi Declarations" and "Assisi Liturgy" please contact either WWF International or WWF UK. There is also the Christian "Winchester Liturgy" available from WWF UK along with school assembly material and service outlines for churches.